COAST GUARD FOLLIES
MY HUMOR IN UNIFORM

KEN SMITH

Copyright © 2007 by Ken Smith

Yeoman House, Inc. trade paperback edition 2007
All rights reserved

This Yeoman House softcover edition of Coast Guard Follies is an original publication. It is published by arrangement with the author.

No part of this book may be used or reproduced in any manner whostsoever without written permission except in the case of brief quotations embodied in critical articles or reviews. For information, address:

Yeoman House, Inc., 10 Old Bulgarmarsh Road, Tiverton, Rhode Island 02878.

Printed in the U.S.A.

ISBN13: 978-0-9754676-8-8
Library of Congress Control Number: 2007932842

Deadicashun

This book is deadicated to my wunderfull wife Charlotte.

She is such a wunderfull spellar, that if she haddent edited my book, you probbably wooden't bee able to reed it. Thats only one off her many ass sets. She all so nose about those punkchewashun "thingies" that make the reeding ezier. They didn't teech those things in the Coast Guard. She hassent scene this part, becuz I wanted it too bee a surprise.

Tanks too Charlotte fore always beeing there four me (and you).

About the Author

Ken Smith was born in Brooklyn, New York, in 1930. He was a "Depression kid." Although his parents were from Rhode Island, Ken grew up in rural western Massachusetts, enjoying an outdoor boyhood.

After his Coast Guard adventures, Ken became an electronics engineer and finally a general foreman at an electronic plant in Worcester, Mass.

His hobbies have always included both ham radio and photography. Most of the photos in this book were taken by the author.

Ken has always believed that keeping one's focus on the humorous side of life is the best way to become a happy person. He certainly lived that philosophy during his year on an isolated island in the Pacifc, exploring the ways of the native peoples and the wildlife on the island. He only wishes more people would look to the funny and happy side of life, rather than the negative. "Looking at life from the bright side is the best way to go!" he says.

Ken and his wife Charlotte moved to Rhode Island in 1976 and live there today.

CHAPTER ONE
In the Beginning

THIS STORY BEGINS in 1947 when I was seventeen years old and a high school junior in Oxford, Mass. I had always lived in this small rural town and enjoyed an outdoor life that included hunting and fishing. My goal in life was to become a wildlife conservation officer.

The University of Massachusetts in Amherst, Mass., offered such a program. But my parents had just finished putting my sister Dot through four years of teachers college and there wasn't much money left for me. I would have to live on campus and the expenses seemed great. In addition, at that time, right after the second World War, all young men still had a military obligation to fill.

One Sunday in church, my sister met a local fellow named Ken Schofield. He was in the U.S. Coast Guard, had just returned from an overseas assignment in the Pacific and was about to be discharged. My sister and Ken began a courtship, during which time he and I became good friends and spent a lot of time together. He was a newly licensed ham radio operator—another interest of mine. We spent many evenings building radio equipment for his ham radio station. During these evenings, Ken and I often discussed my future and college plans. He thought that I should do my military duty first

Coast Guard Follies

and recommended the Coast Guard. Because of my interest and knowledge of radio and electronics, he maintained that I would easily qualify for the Coast Guard's top rated electronics school.

In the fall of 1948, my sister Dot and Ken married and moved to California to start their life. Dot got a job at Glendale College, a junior college in the UCLA system. She wrote to tell me that if I moved in with them I could attend Glendale College tuition free for two years and then transfer to UCLA, also tuition free, as I would then satisfy the residency requirements. That certainly sounded like an easy solution to my education problems so I never made any other applications to any local colleges. That turned out to have been a mistake.

After about nine months, we received a letter from Dot and Ken saying they were fed up with California and were coming home. There went my college plans right down the tubes! So I had to resort to plan B, which was a military assignment.

I started checking out the local recruiting centers, Air Force, Army, and Navy. I didn't like anything they promised, so I met with the Coast Guard and eventually signed on the dotted line.

Within a few weeks I received my notice to appear in Boston for my pre-induction physical. About five days before my trip to Boston I badly sprained my ankle playing football. The day my Dad drove me to Boston for my physical, my ankle was tightly wrapped in an Ace bandage and I could barely walk.

While Dad sat cooling his heels in the waiting area, I went through the damnedest medical procedure I had ever been through. There were about 25 of us potential recruits. First, we were told to strip. Then a Pharmacist Mate * (see glossary) painted a number on each of our chests with orange Methiolate. The doctor checked and probed every orifice he could find on our bodies as he progressed down the line.

I remember that he told the first guy in line to bend over and spread his cheeks. This guy bent over and stuck two fingers in the sides of his mouth and spread those cheeks into a large smile. The pharmacist mate said "No, do your other two cheeks"! I'm glad I

In the Beginning

wasn't the first one in line because I'd have probably done the same thing.

The final test was a foot examination. We were lined up shoulder to shoulder and the Doctor came down the line looking at our feet and saying things like "O.K.", "Out...hammer toes", "Out....flat feet", etc. When he got to me I heard the fateful words, "Out...flat feet". I was devastated! Those of us who had been disqualified were told to put on our clothes and go home.

Now, I had never been a very aggressive person, but this was serious so I decided to go for broke. When everyone else was gone I went to the doctor's desk and told him I never had any problems with flat feet. Indeed, I had run on the cross country track team in high school and never had any problems with my feet.

He said, "What's your name, son"? He found my application forms in the pile on his desk and looked it over. "Smith, I see you were born in Brooklyn, New York," he said. "Well, so was I. So I'm going to give you another chance. Take off your shoes, socks, and that ace bandage, and walk away from me."

I did that as best I could. Then he said, "Turn around and walk towards me on your tip toes." I took one step and about fell on my face from the pain. He said," If you can't do that, then I can't accept you. But because we're both from Brooklyn, I'll give you thirty days for your ankle to get better and we'll try it again."

I thanked him but I thought I was just being let down easy. I never thought he'd let me come back and try again. The trip home with my Dad was mostly silent.

But sure enough, about twenty days later an official envelope from the Coast Guard arrived and I was scheduled for another physical. The new trip to Boston and the repeat physical was exactly the same except for the foot inspection. As before, the Doc came down the line of recruits, uttering the same things he did the first time, except this time when he got to me he just said, "O.K." and looked at me for a split second with a slight smile. I was in. This time the trip home with Dad was all talk.

About a month later, I was ordered to report to Boston for induction and transportation to Cape May, New Jersey, for boot camp training. When that day came, Mom and Dad again took me to Boston. We said our farewells and I boarded a train to New York's Penn Station and then on to Cape May. I was traveling with two other Boston-area recruits.

CHAPTER TWO
Boot Camp

THE JOURNEY FROM Boston to Cape May was my first trip on a train. After the stop at Penn Station in New York, we headed to Philadelphia. We arrived about 9 p.m. and were told that the train to Cape May didn't leave until 8 the next morning. We spent the whole night hanging around the station and almost went nuts!

At dawn the next morning we decided to go outside for some fresh air. What a mistake that was. The smell was nauseating. It smelled like rotten meat or something worse. How anyone could live with that smell all the time is beyond me. I never found out what the source of the foul odor was. Maybe it had something to do with the meat packing industry in that area.

Finally we boarded the train to Cape May, New Jersey. That trip was something out of an old western movie. It was a "local" train, so we stopped at every village station, shack, or milk can along the way. After each stop we'd begin to pick up speed and then immediately start to slow down again and the conductor would pass through the cars announcing the name of the next stop. I'll always remember him saying, "Tuckahoe Junction, Tuck...a...hoe!"

Cape May is the end of the line and it seemed to take forever to get there. When we got off the train, there was a gray school bus

Coast Guard Follies

waiting for us. It was a short trip to the Coast Guard Training Center.

We were then ushered into our temporary barracks, which was one of the older, old fashioned, gray, wooden, two-story buildings in the complex. Everything else was painted white. We were told to pick a bunk. I don't remember what we had for bedding. Over the next two or three days other recruits continued to arrive until there were enough of us to form a "company."

We were not allowed to wander outside a fifteen-foot perimeter from our barracks. There was a small "smoking area" just outside, as smoking was not allowed in the barracks. This is when we were taught how to "Field Strip" * (see glossary) a cigarette. You really can't do that today because modern cigarettes have filters on them, unlike the ones from the old days. We were marched to the mess hall, which was only about 100 feet away, three times a day We were told to salute anything that had gold on it and if you weren't sure, salute anyway.

On my second day there, we were marched to a supply building where we got our first clothing issue, which consisted of underwear, chambray shirts, tee shirts, dungarees, white hats, socks, shoes, blankets, mattress covers (fart sacks), and a sea bag to store everything in. We were then told to strip down and and don our new Coast Guard clothes, and to place all our clothes and personal belongings in cardboard boxes for shipping home.

Now came the fun. We were moved to the second floor of our barracks and instructed on how to stencil every piece of gear we had just been issued. And it had to be done exactly right. We were given a very stiff bristle brush, a glob of black gooey paint, and a stencil of the data that was to be placed in a very precise place on each item. One poor guy named Bospisle wasn't listening too well and stenciled his data on the outside brim of his white hats. He was told to scrub it off! Of course, the ink was indelible, so he spent hours scrubbing away with no results. I don't know what kind of ink it was, but 56 years later my name and serial number are still legible on my old laundry bag, even after thousands of washings. They sure made things good in those days.

Boot Camp

Next came another physical exam, exactly like the one I had in Boston, and again they checked our feet last of all. The pharmacist mate who was doing the exam saw my feet and said, "Smith, how the hell did you get here"? I played dumb and asked "What's the problem"?

He replied, "Your feet are as flat as pancakes, that's what, and if you ever want to get out of the Coast Guard just go to the nearest officer and tell him your feet hurt. You'll be on your way home immediately." I thought that was a useful piece of information to file away, but I never had to use it. Even today, I can say my flat feet have never caused me a big problem!

Eventually we became known as company G-5 and moved to our permanent barracks, one of the newest on the base. Our company commander was "Commander Ford." He was a vanishing breed in the Coast Guard because his rate was a Petty Officer First Class "Surfman,"*(see glossary) which was a carry over from the old Surf Stations along the coast.

Everything we owned, except our bedding and our pea coats, was stored in our sea bags, hung by their ropes on a long rail down the center of the barracks. We had no lockers, so getting into or out of our stuff was a chore.

Soon the serious training started. It seemed to us that the Coast Guard was a "marching" outfit rather than a sea-going one because it seemed that's all we did all day. Marching and "close order" drills with an M-1* (see glossary) were our daily constants, no matter what other training we had scheduled. But even after three months of marching and drills, there were still a number of recruits who never seemed to know their right foot from their left or their rear from their front!

"Life Boat" training was next on the list. We were marched down to the boat docks and introduced to the 26-foot Monomoy Surf Boat*. These monsters were propelled by ten oarsmen and a coxswain*. The oars were about twelve feet long and weighed a ton. We didn't have oar locks, per se, but two wooden pins.

Watching our company first attempt to row these behemoths was funnier than the Three Stooges. Most of our guys were from the city, the Midwest, or the rural south, and had never been in a boat. Certainly, few had ever pulled an oar. Because I was from New England and had been around boats all my life, this was a piece of cake for me and I was eventually selected to be on our company race boat crew as the "stroke." The stroke oarsman is the rower upon whom the rest of the crew synchronizes.

Somewhere along about the end of January, we were marched down to the long pier on the harbor for more life boat training. Cape May is not a place I'd choose to be in the middle of winter. It was very cold. We got very little snow, but lots of cold rain. The only clothes we had were the dungarees, chambray shirts, pea coats, and regulation leather shoes we had been issued. They didn't even give us any warm foul-weather jackets or boots. We certainly weren't dressed for outdoors training, six hours a day.

The "drill" that cold day was to teach us how to lower one of those 26-foot surfboat monsters from a ship at sea, with eleven people on board, using the old fashioned rope and pulley davits. The company was divided into three groups, one group in the boat, and two groups to man the lines.

Because I was on the "race boat" crew, I was one of the "lucky" eleven to be assigned to the boat. Everything went smoothly as we were slowly lowered some twenty feet down toward the water.

When the boat was about six or seven feet above the water, Commander Ford gave the order to "HOLD." He then started a lecture about launching a life boat in a rough sea. He explained that you have to time things right so the boat lands on the top of a wave. The object is to literally drop the boat very quickly on a wave crest. The command for this maneuver is "UP ENDS." Cape May harbor doesn't have any waves but we were going to do it anyway.

Apparently, the crew tending the davit line for the bow of the life boat got bored with the lecture and stopped paying attention. When the command "UP ENDS" came, they were out to lunch, while the stern crew acted flawlessly. The stern dropped beautifully, but the bow stayed right where it was. My end of the boat struck the ice cold water with a mighty splash. The coxswain and

Boot Camp

two or three others got pitched overboard. Those in the bow came tumbling down towards the stern. It was another sight straight out of a "Three Stooges" movie! We fished the dunked "boots" out of the water and back in the boat. Just about everybody was wet. They hauled us back up to the dock level and we were "double timed" back to the barracks.

We didn't see Commander Ford for the rest of the day. I think he was in his office writing his transfer request.

During my three months of boot camp training there were other memorable weeks. One week we pulled mess hall duty where we learned to peel potatoes, wash dishes and do other important kitchen jobs. I suppose you have to train those guys with the two left feet to be useful for something.

Another week we had guard duty. Every hour we stood watches on various parts of the base. For 24 hours a day, in four-hour shifts, we guarded everything on the base from the barracks, sick bay, main gate, boat dock, South West Gate, to the O.D.'s*(see glossary) orderly.

For some reason, I always seemed to get the best assignments. Some of the guys were assigned to the power station coal pile, shoveling coal for four hours and came back to the barracks filthy. I never got any of those nasty jobs, except for the boat dock guard. This involved patrolling not only the boat dock and aircraft hanger area, but also the edge of the living quarters area. It was a very remote part of the base. You had to punch a watchman's type recording time clock that was hung over your shoulder, at very precise times, every fifteen minutes at specific stations.

My life saving routine was to make a clock punch, run like hell to a very small, warm, steam-distribution shack that leaked steam, watch the clock, run to the next time punch station, run back to the steam shack, etc., etc. The only problem was that due to the very cold weather my outer clothes would be covered with ice from the condensed steam.

Some of the recruits were assigned to the South West Gate. This was the furthest corner of the base where the chain link fence surrounding the base ran out into the ocean. There was a tiny guard shack and that's all. They brought the recruit guard down there in a jeep and left him there for four hours. He also had to punch a time clock every fifteen minutes.

However, therein lies the legend of South West Annie. She was a young lady that would come up to the fence during the night and provide the guard with sexual favors through the fence. I was never fortunate enough to draw that duty assignment. So maybe I didn't get all the good assignments. I never have figured out how Commander Ford made the assignments he did and why I always seemed to get the good duty. Maybe it was because I knew my right foot from my left.

Another guard outpost was the "Lookout Tower". It was a small unheated room, windows all around, perched atop a 40-foot steel tower. It was very much like a fire lookout tower. The tower watch guard was required to report everything that moved to the O.D. by telephone.

We reported every boat, plane, sea gull, we could see, for fear that he would have seen it and we didn't report it. I always pitied that poor O.D. for his telephone chores. His answer to our report was always, "Very well". I was fortunate that I was only assigned that duty during the night hours when you couldn't see too much. But it sure was cold up there!

Inspections were held every Saturday and that required that we scrupulously clean our barracks, washing and rolling all our clothes, laying out our entire sea bag contents on our bunks in the prescribed manner, with a "Captain's Inspection" in the aircraft hanger. Washing and hanging out clothes was a problem in the middle of winter in Cape May. They almost always froze. Somehow most of us were able to do it.

There was one nice thing about those inspections. All week long, we were required to wear canvas leggings, but on Thursday night we were allowed to remove them so we could scrub them for Saturday's inspection. It sure was nice to get those damn tight things off our legs, even if just for one day.

The personnel inspections in the aircraft hanger caused me a problem one very cold Saturday. We were practicing the close order

Boot Camp

drill with our M-1's rifles and I slammed the bolt closed, right on my thumb. Oh my! In that really cold hanger it hurt so bad I could barely hold the gun.

After suffering through all the problems of boot camp for eight weeks we were allowed "liberty" on Sundays. It began with a 10 a.m. inspection to make sure that we were correctly dressed to meet the public as proper Coast Guardsmen. We then boarded the Gray Bus for the trip to downtown Cape May.

There was a nice USO facility on the huge boardwalk that bordered the ocean and that's where the girls were. The girls were not allowed to leave the building with a sailor so there wasn't any hanky-panky under the board walk. (Damn!!) In retrospect I suppose that was smart because who would want their teenage daughter cavorting with a horny teen age boy who had been cooped up for eight weeks. This one simple rule probably prevented a population explosion in Cape May.

The Gray Bus returned to the base at 4 P.M., but that short liberty was nice.

There were a few weirdoes in our company. One was Dardener. He was so proud of his penis, he would walk around the barracks with his "thing" in his hand for all to admire. Sometimes he would approach a guy laying in his bunk, and bonk him on the head with his marvelous appendage.

One night he made a big mistake. He bonked Stacy Madwick on the head with it. Now Stacy was a genuine hillbilly from the Carolina mountains. Stacy wrote to his Pappy every night with a green fountain pen. When Dardener bonked him, Stacy stopped his writing and stabbed Dardener's penis with his green pen.

I don't think Dardener ever bonked anyone again for the rest of boot camp. But his green tattoo was still there when we left. I always wondered how he explained that to his future sexual partners.

After three months, we were nearing graduation day. We had to take "final exams" to determine what our qualifications were and where we would be assigned in the next phase of our Coast Guard careers. This testing took a couple of days. When the results were in, I was told by a yeoman that I didn't qualify for ET* (see glossary) school because I didn't score high enough on the spelling exam. However, he said I was qualified to attend radioman's school.

I was devastated! I called home that night really upset. Mom tried to console me and told me I could be the best radioman the Coast Guard ever had. Yeah right! That's not what I joined up for!

A few days later we were interviewed by a couple of officers and they asked me why I had opted for radioman's school instead of electronics school. I told them what the yeoman had told me and they said, "Smith, you're going to ET school." I couldn't wait to get to the telephone to tell my folks. I was back on cloud nine.

At the end of three fast-paced months, graduation day finally arrived. After the normal ceremonies and picture taking, we would have a home leave and then head to our new duty stations as seamen second class. The next day the Gray Bus took us to the Cape May train station for the train trip to Philadelphia. There, we all went our separate ways, me to New York and Boston and eventually back home to Rochdale, Mass., with my sea bag over my shoulder. I had ten days leave before reporting to Groton, Conn., for six months of Electronic School.

CHAPTER THREE
Electronics School

BEFORE I ENLISTED in the Coast Guard I was involved in the Youth Fellowship group in my church. At the age of eighteen I was the oldest "youth' in the group. One night, at one of our meetings, there was a young lady named Eartha who absolutely had to be home by nine p.m., even though she was at a church function. Normally, one of her neighbors would walk her home after the meeting, but on this night everyone was having so much fun that he didn't want to leave at nine.

As oldest in the group, I thought it would be good to teach these young lads a lesson about chivalry. So I said, "Eartha, I'll walk you home!" And I did. She even kissed me good night for my efforts. That chivalrous act made Eartha and me an "item." It was all quite innocent, but she did write to me frequently while I was at boot camp.

When I came home for my ten days leave, I looked forward to seeing Eartha, even if she still had to be home by 9 p.m. I really didn't mind the early curfew, since I was short of money. I saw nothing wrong with a date that was short and cheap!

The ten days leave just flew by and it was soon time to leave for Groton, Conn. for Electronics School. My folks drove me down.

Coast Guard Follies

This "base" was the grandest place you could imagine. It looked like a high-priced college campus, with beautiful landscaping, modern dormitory buildings, and granite pillars and wrought iron gates. The administration building looked like a mansion. I was assigned to a temporary dorm while we waited for the other students to arrive.

There were about thirty of us and we moved to our permanent dorm, two students to each room. Each room had two bunks, a study table, and clothing lockers. It was a far cry from the conditions at boot camp.

The electronics course was intense, covering basic electronic theory, practical experience and theory dealing with radio transmitters, receivers, Radar, Sonar, and Loran.* In effect, we received a two year college education in six months. Classes started at 8 a.m. and continued until 4 p.m., with a break for lunch, and most serious students spent two or three hours doing homework every night. We were allowed liberty every weekend from 4:30 p.m. on Friday until Monday morning, unless we had a dormitory security watch.

I always hitchhiked home for weekends but I had to take a bus out of the New London area because the shore patrol* would not allow hitch-hiking. In those days a sailor beside the road with his thumb out could always get a ride. The only problem was that I always seemed to get rides from gays! I once conned one of them to take me almost all the way home. At a gas station where my folks always picked me up, I told him I had to take a leak. He said he did too. The poor guy was devastated when I got out his car with just a polite thank you.

Although I was in school for the academics, one of the most important things I learned about was the Italian grinder. Most weekday evenings, one of the guys would visit our dorm rooms and take our snack orders. We lived on grinders and a Coke—75 cents! They delivered them to the main gate in a large cardboard box and someone brought them up to the dorm. These sandwiches were monsters by today's standards. They were at least a foot long and loaded with all the normal meats, cheese, lettuce and tomatoes, and grinder sauce.

Electronics School

The food at the school was really pretty good. In fact, one Friday I walked down the chow line and found the entree that day was boiled lobster. As I sat at the mess table tearing into my dinner, I looked across the table where a classmate from Missouri was staring at his lobster, poking it confusedly with a fork. I asked what was wrong and he answered, "My God, I don't know who's going to eat who!"

He gave up and put his lobster on my tray. I heard someone else say, "Give it to Smith. He'll eat it." I ate about six lobsters that day. Those Midwest boys just never understood New England's finest delicacy!

We did have one culinary tragedy the night they served some tainted hot dogs. Most of the school was sick. There was vomit all over the dorm, even plastered on the window screens where guys tried to puke out the windows. The whole place reeked. The sick bay did a booming business.

The only other "bad" food I remember was "S.O.S" (Shit on a Shingle), otherwise known as creamed, chipped beef. Actually, it wasn't bad, if it was made the way it was supposed to be made, but if they substituted hamburger for the chipped beef, it was truly awful!

Another near tragedy happened in one of our classes. One of our instructors was almost as big as his native Texas. He was demonstrating something in an open transmitter while holding a metal microphone in his hand. He touched the wrong thing and got zapped and went flying across the room, scattering desks and students in his path. He was stunned and embarrassed, and that was the end of class for that day.

On June 25th, 1950 a real tragedy began: the Korean War. It was sobering news for those of us in the military, as was the background context of the Cold War. We realized that we could be in the front lines of a real shooting war.

Also that year we read in the newspaper that somebody at Bell Labs had invented something called a transistor. Someone predicted that one day transistors would replace the vacuum tubes that were in all electronic gear in those days. We all laughed. Of course, it was true, and the transistor not only changed the world, but played a large part of my later civilian life.

In August our training was over. I graduated third in my class. The school hierarchy wanted me to stay on as an instructor, but that is not what I wanted. So, as I requested, I was sent to the First Coast Guard District in Boston. What assignment they had for me, I had no idea.

We graduated on a Friday and now proudly sported our new Third Class Petty Officer's "crows" on our left sleeve. The next day, driving back to campus in my Dad's car to pick up my stuff, I was pulled over for speeding. When the cop came up to my car window, he said "In a hurry sailor?"

"Yes sir," I said. "I'm on my way back to the base and I really have to take a wicked crap!"

He pushed his cap back on his head and managed not to laugh out loud. "Okay, son," he said, "But try and keep it down a bit." I'll bet my excuse was all over the station house that night.

After ten days leave at home, I reported to Boston.

CHAPTER FOUR
Duty in the North Atlantic

AFTER ANOTHER TEN wonderful days of leave, I traveled to Boston by train and reported to the Coast Guard First District headquarters on Atlantic Ave. The 1st Coast Guard District encompassed essentially all of New England, from Connecticut to Maine. And that included all the Coast Guard operations that took place in that area, from "Ocean Station Vessels" that plied the high seas, to small harbor boats, life boat stations, radar stations, and rescue aircraft.

I was again "in transit" and assigned a bunk on the transient floor of the barracks. After an interview with an officer I was assigned to the Coast Guard Cutter Humboldt -- a 311 foot long Ocean Station Vessel otherwise known as a weather ship. She plied the North Atlantic but weather reporting was only a small part of her duty. Because she was in Baltimore for some repairs, I had about a week to wait for my ship to arrive and I spent that time in the base electronic repair shop.

Finally my ship came in. With sea bag over my shoulder I walked down the pier to where the Humboldt was moored, climbed the gangway, saluted the Colors and the quarter deck, as I had been taught, and handed my orders to the Officer of the Deck. He told me to go to the ship's office for my berthing assignment. There were a bunch of scruffy looking Coasties lounging around the quarter deck and I asked them "How do you get to the ship's office?" They replied in unison, "You walk!" So much for a warm welcome.

I found my way to the Engineering Quarters, picked a vacant lower bunk, and stowed my gear in a nearby locker. That sounds easy but I had never been on a ship before and didn't know the bow from the stern, or where anything important was, like the "head" (bathroom), mess deck, or electronic shop. I soon met my Chief ET, and as luck would have it his name was also Smith. The other member of the electronics crew was petty officer second class Don Everton. Over the next few weeks, while the ship was in port, Don took me under his wing and I learned the layout of my ship while performing routine maintenance on all types of electronic gear. I was beginning to feel like a salty dog. How little I knew what a real salty dog was.

Liberty was every day at 4:30 p.m. and you didn't have to be back until "Quarters" (roll call) the next morning at 8 a.m. Boston was a great liberty city. The Old Howard Vaudeville and Burlesque Theater was still there in Scully Square. It wasn't just a stripper joint and I saw many of the old vaudevillian actors and comics that eventually became movie and television stars. I enjoyed the antics of the likes of Bob Hope, Jack Benny & Gracie Allen, Peg Leg Bates, Gypsy Rose Lee, and many others.

There was a Howard Johnson's restaurant called "H J's" on Boylston Street that the Humboldt "elite" had adopted as their own and we renamed it the "Humboldt Junction", after the name of our ship. The restaurant was on the ground floor and the bar was located upstairs on a surrounding balcony.

The bartender's name was Jose and he introduced me to the "Side Car" cocktail and a few others. This was not a rowdy place at all. In those days, if you were old enough to serve your country, you were old enough to drink, no matter what your actual age. I was never refused a drink while I was in uniform. Only the "best" petty officers and commissioned officers from the Humboldt gathered there.

Duty in the North Atlantic

Every other storefront in Scully Square seemed to be a tattoo parlor, and I just had to have one. After all, what kind of a salty sailor doesn't have a tattoo? So one night I walked up Hanover Street to Scully Square, picked out a tattoo parlor and got an anchor with a Coast Guard banner tattooed on my right biceps. Boy, I was getting saltier by the day! I'm surprised I didn't die from that experience because they didn't use the sterile procedures like they do today.

I also learned that even though Boston has a huge Italian population, they didn't know how to make an Italian grinder! At least, not like the ones we had enjoyed in Groton, Norwich, New London!

Because I lived only about fifty miles to the west of Boston I could get home on weekends and even sometimes just for an overnight visit. Again I mostly got around by hitch hiking, after getting out of town to avoid the Shore Patrol. During my frequent trips home, Eartha, the girl with the 9 p.m. curfew, was always there waiting for me.

After a few weeks, we left Boston for my first North Atlantic "weather patrol" on Station Charlie, which is in the mid North Atlantic south of Greenland. I didn't have any idea what an ordeal this was going to be and I had no idea about the fact that the autumn is hurricane season in that part of the world.

These patrols usually consisted of thirty days on station, plus the five days to get there and five days to return to port, for an average of forty days at sea. We would stay in port for about fifty days and then head back to sea to do it all over again.

We hadn't been at sea for long before the pangs of sea sickness began to affect me. I never actually barfed, but I sure felt like I could. In a few days it went away, only to return periodically when the seas got progressively rougher.

One day I heard over the PA system, "Now hear this, Now hear this, Smith ET3, lay up to CIC". The Combat Information Center (CIC) is where most of the electronic equipment of the ship is installed. When I got there, Chief Smith & ET2 Everton were already there working on the fathometer, which had stopped working. This monster piece of equipment was a relic from World War II and stood six feet high and three feet wide, with a very large glass dial, marked around its circumference with depth readings. An orange neon light flashed at zero and also flashed at the depth under the keel. At least that was what it was supposed to do. The Captain was pacing around CIC, with an ever-present cigar clamped in his teeth.

After some preliminary checks, we determined that there was something wrong with the drive motor for the rotary neon light, we decided to replace the motor. I was sent down to the hold to fetch a spare from the spare parts box.

To replace this part we had to remove the holding screws and the retaining clips for the large glass dial cover. When the new motor was in place, my job was to hold the glass dial in place while we tested the new motor. So far, so good. Then, someone needed a tool, so, trying to be helpful, I bent down to get it from the tool box. The ship rolled and there was a tremendous crash and the glass dial I was supposed to be holding smashed in a gazillion pieces on the deck. There was a very brief stunned silence. I said something very professional, like, "Oops!"

The Captain glared at me and chomped down on his cigar. I was mortified! Not a great way to impress the Captain on my first patrol.

As it turned out, that dial was the only part for which we didn't have a spare. So now we had no "bottom eyes." I can't imagine what difference it would make. We were in 2,000 fathoms of water (about 12,000 feet) and in no danger of going aground.

One of the Chief Machinist Mates spent a full day making a paper replacement, using a picture from the fathometer service manual. God rest that man's soul! We finished the patrol, didn't run aground, and everyone forgot about my blunder except me and maybe the Captain. (In 1994 I sent to the National Archives for a copy of my official service record. There was no mention of my blunder. King Neptune was kind to me!)

The North Atlantic in the fall or winter is no place any sane human should be. Next to Hell I can't imagine a worse place. All east coast storms of any sort--hurricanes, Nor'easters, or anything else--curve up there due to the influence of the Gulf Stream's northeastward flow. And that's where this patrol was stationed. The wind and resulting fifty-foot waves are beyond description. If you saw the Humboldt in Boston, tied up to the dock, you would think it was a rather big ship. In the wild North Atlantic it was nothing but a 311-foot cork.

For days on end, it was all one could do to just stand up without getting hurt. One day we rolled forty-seven degrees and I didn't think we were ever going to straighten up. There were times when you could have walked up the bulkheads (walls) as easily as the decks. You could not go out on a weather deck without getting washed away. In such conditions, sea sickness was normal, in one degree or another, for much of the crew. There was one poor young seaman who was so sick he was at death's door. Fortunately, a petty officer came down with appendicitis at the same time. So we received permission to leave the Ocean Station and proceed to Argentia, Newfoundland, the closest point of land. While enroute to Newfoundland another crew member also came down with appendicitis so we had three crewmen to off-load. I'm sure getting into calmer waters was a blessing to them and the rest of the crew as well. We off-loaded the sick and proceeded back to Station "Charlie".

The normal routine for joining up with the other ship that was "on station", or coming to relieve us, was to keep at least a mile apart. We kept track of each other by radar. We would load up all the mail, movies and other gear in covered life rafts and launch it over the side, with a radar reflector. Then, we'd pull away from the raft and let the other ship intercept it. They'd take it aboard, remove the contents, reload with their mail and reverse the process.

While we were near the other ship, a joint "Rawin" (high altitude radio weather balloon) launch was conducted with both ships tracking it so we could compare results. When all was done, they departed for home and we were officially in charge of the Ocean Station.

Aside from weather observations we had other duties. One of our principal responsibilities was tracking and providing radar position reports to all transatlantic aircraft. Remember, in the 1950's there were no satellites or global positioning receivers, so this was the state of the art, as primitive as it was. We also were allowed to leave the station in the event of a rescue at sea. We also functioned as radio direction transmitting station. In those days that was one of the major position-determining methods for ships and planes, along with Loran.

As an electronics technician I was one of the few petty officers on the ship who didn't stand watches. It wasn't long before I was dubbed "Rackets." I had free run of the ship, and pretty much was in control of my own routine, except for electronic emergencies.

I spent much of my time in the radio room, CIC, or the radar room and the latter was a real delight often in the wee hours of the night. If the transatlantic flight we were tracking and communicating with by radio had a celebrity aboard, the pilot would often invite them to the cockpit to talk to us poor swabbies. I had many conversations with movie stars and they always asked what the hell we were doing down there. I always said the correct thing and never said that I didn't have the foggiest idea. I could stay up this late at night because Everton, the other ET, would answer up for me at "Quarters" the next morning while I was "sleeping in" due to a late night duty call.

Eventually our thirty days on station was up and we were relieved by another ship and headed back to Boston. Once, off the coast of Nova Scotia, we were sent on a rescue mission for a foundering coal ship. By the time we got there it was too late. The cargo had shifted and the ship had capsized and sunk. There was nothing left except the wooden pilot house that was still floating and some scattered debris. It was deemed to be a hazard to navigation and we were ordered to destroy it by gunfire. Although we were a fully equipped fighting ship, complete with a five-inch deck gun, 20 and 40 mm anti-aircraft guns, depth charges, K-guns, and hedgehogs, destroying that pilot house proved to be a challenge. All the guns could do was punch holes in it but it just kept floating. So we rammed it and broke it into a thousand pieces.

We finally arrived in Boston and liberty was declared for the

Duty in the North Atlantic

non-watch sections of the crew. I walked up Hanover Street to the subway station like a drunken sailor. Forty days on rough seas will do that to you because your brain still thinks the world is flopping around.

     Because it was hunting season, another shipmate and I took ten days leave to get in some bird hunting. We stayed at my house and my Mom was glad to have us home and enjoyed hearing our sea stories.

CHAPTER FIVE
Ocean Station Easy

MY SHIPMATE ARNE and I spent our leave hunting and chasing girls. I had gotten hooked up with the daughter of some close friends of my parents. Her name was Fancy and she lived in North Providence, Rhode Island. That was about forty miles from my home in central Massachusetts so it made getting together a bit difficult. After a few excursions to Rhode Island in Dad's car it became clear I needed my own transportation.

So I bought my first car. It was a 1939 Plymouth four door only about eleven years old. In those days cars were built like tanks. That made the commute to Providence a lot easier. I could even do it from Boston. What about "nine p.m. curfew" Eartha? I'm ashamed to admit I told her that most weekends I had "the duty," and she'd just have to get used to having a sailor for a boyfriend. She never figured out that I was two-timing her. Eartha wasn't smart enough to figure this out, which we shall see later.

From third grade on, I always had a girlfriend. Joan, Nancy, Lucille (two of them, in fact), June, Hope, Diana, Mary Lou, Jeannine and more I've probably forgotten. But Eartha was my first "serious" girlfriend, and after her came Fancy from Providence. I can honestly say, quoting our recent President, "I never had sex with those women!" But, like President Clinton, I suppose that depends on how you define "sex."

"Providence Fancy" was the strangest girl I ever knew. I could not touch her with my hands below her neck or above her knees, but she would kiss me like she was about to rape me. Her advertising was good but you couldn't touch the "goods."

When my leave was over it was back to the Humboldt in Boston. While she was in port I had a variety of duties to perform. Aside from the obvious electronic maintenance there were many other chores to tend to. Some of the petty officers on duty during the day were also assigned to Shore Patrol duty in the evening hours. Along with men from other service branches, we were the military "cops" for Boston. We patrolled the city watching for wayward sailors. If you didn't draw a street patrol you were assigned to the "Riot Squad" and cooled your heels at the Joy Street police station until you were called upon to put down a commotion or brawl somewhere in the city.

I remember one in particular. We left the police station in the paddy wagon and arrived at a bar on Washington Street. There was a full blown riot going on inside. As we entered the front door, a sailor about twice as big as me, came at me with a chair raised over his head ready to bust me up good. I dropped to the deck and smacked him across the shin bones with my night stick. He fell in a heap, howling in pain and swearing at me like you wouldn't believe. I'm sure that shot to the shins hurt like hell but it was him or me. We cuffed them all and took them back to the jail. Some patrols were a walk in the park, but the ones on Washington Street were among the worst. Today, of course, that part of downtown Boston is known as the "Combat Zone," and for good reason.

Another port duty was marching in parades for the various holidays. This was not my idea of choice duty in the middle of the winter. The actual marching in the parade itself was a welcome relief after hours of standing around on a side street waiting for the cue to begin marching..

During one of our port layovers, the electronic department was scheduled to get steel shelving installed in the bowels of the ship down at keel level, where all our spare parts boxes were stored. This would enable us to better organize our spare parts operation.

The work was to be done by the civilian dock workers and a happy-go-lucky group they were. As the low man on the "ET" roster, my job was standing the fire watch, while these guys shot welding sparks all over the place. All went well for a time. When they found out I was interested in learning to weld, they were more than happy to let me don a welding face shield and have at it, while they did the heavy supervising.

One day, while I was standing fire watch duties (I wasn't welding) there was a mighty whoosh and we suddenly had a bilge fire. The brave welders all yelled "Let's get the Hell out of here!" and they did. That left me to deal with the problem. As they all disappeared up the ladder, out of the compartment, I yelled, "Get some help!" The fire was under the deck plates, in the bilge spaces, and I quickly discovered that most of the deck plates were welded in place.

By now the flames were shooting up from many of the small places between the plates, but none of those places were big enough to get the horn on my fire extinguisher to the fire. Flames were squirting up where the deck plates met the bulkhead and it suddenly dawned on me that on the other side of that bulkhead was the powder magazine! That put a whole new slant on the problem!

I found one or two deck plates that had apparently come loose in the past and had been repaired by screwing them down. I took one of the welders crow bars and pried up the edge enough to get the extinguisher horn in there and "let 'er rip". It was working, and a good thing, because by now I was really scared! The problem was that the ship had fore and aft ribs and I was only getting CO_2 in one alley. So I started prying other plates up and doused those spaces too.

Eventually, I had things pretty much under control. That's when the fire brigade showed up and began telling me how to put the fire out. It all ended well. I saved the ship, didn't get a medal, and nobody even said "thank you." Go figure!

Ocean Station Easy

Because I had been raised in a rural community I wasn't very sophisticated and didn't know squat about a lot of things. Coast Guard life sure added to my informal education. For example, I had visions of getting married and making the military a career. I soon changed my mind about the military career part of that.

Don, the other Electronics technician, was married and had a new baby. He and his wife were from some other part of the country and were living in a cheap apartment somewhere in Boston. The amount of money the government paid us just wasn't enough to support that lifestyle even as meager as it was. Don was always borrowing money from me "just until pay day."

I was single and had no big financial obligations so I was happy to help him out. He always paid me back. Because of my status as a "near home" sailor, I wanted weekends at home. The other guys took their liberty any time they could get it until they ran out of money. I parlayed this into a good deal for me. A few days after payday, when they were flush, I would stand their watches for them. But they would owe me. When they ran out of money for liberty, they would pay me back and stand my watches, and of course I always called in those I.O.U.'s on weekends so I could go home.

At the end of December we were scheduled to go to Ocean Station Easy. This patrol sounded like a gift from King Neptune because Station Easy was in the middle of the Atlantic around 700 miles northeast of Bermuda. Compared to the far North Atlantic, this patrol should really be "easy."

Two nights before we left, I found myself at HJ's (the Humboldt Junction). Jose the bartender and the pretty hostess were sad to learn we were about to leave. About midnight one of the young ensigns from the ship showed up with a Christmas tree to take back to the ship. After a few more cocktails it was time for us to get back. We were standing at the top of the stairs that led down to the main dining room saying our goodbyes and Merry Christmas to everyone. The ensign handed me the Christmas tree to hold while he kissed the hostess. The next thing I knew she was kissing me. I was so surprised I took a step backward, and still holding the Christmas tree, went tumbling down the stairs. Fortunately I didn't get hurt but the people in the dining room got a laugh. I'm sure some of them thought, "just another drunken sailor." They probably were right but did you ever see one with a Christmas tree? The ensign paid for the cab ride back to the ship. On the day before Christmas, we left Boston and the miserable cold and snowy weather.

We headed due east and in twenty-four hours were basking in the bright sunshine and 70 degree temperatures of the Gulf Stream. Most New Englanders have no idea how close that type of balmy weather is and neither did I. On Christmas Day we had a thunder storm. Most days the off-duty crew sunbathed on the quarter deck after noon chow. The seas were generally calm, as compared to the North Atlantic and that made for a much better patrol than Station Charlie. The sea was full of marine creatures like dolphins, sharks, giant squid, and many types of sea birds. We also saw other ships passing, which almost never happened in the far North Atlantic. In fact on Christmas Day we passed another ship which sent us "Happy Holidays" on their blinker light.

We finally arrived on station and relieved the Cutter Mendota. Because the seas were so calm, this time we could actually see the other ship. After the normal life-raft transfer of mail and movies, we were now Ocean Station Easy.

On New Year's Eve all hell broke loose. We blew or rang every noise maker on the ship: whistles, horns, sirens, and bells. Nobody else heard it out there in that vast ocean but it was a good boost for the crew. On another evening someone played "Taps" on a harmonica at ten p.m. I don't know whether that was a breach of military discipline or not but it sure went over big with the crew.

The weather and the seas were so calm we spent a lot of time just laying on station, rather than being under way all the time. There were sharks all over the place and huge four foot long squid. In the late evening we would turn on one of our search lights and shine it down into the water alongside. This would attract the plankton and the small fish, which in turn would attract larger predator fish and squid.

Because the weather was very nice I spent a lot of time in the evenings fishing. I tried using hot dogs for bait but the sharks

Ocean Station Easy

apparently didn't know hot dogs were tasty, because I never caught one. There were dolphins all over the ocean. I used to go up and hang over the bow and watch them surf in our bow wave. With their smiling faces they looked like they could be your friend.

I was also able to do some shooting with the hunting rifle that the Captain had allowed me to have aboard. I always saved the defunct electronic tubes I replaced on the ship because they made good targets floating in the sea. On any nice calm Sunday afternoon I would be out there on the quarter deck with my rifle entertaining the crew with my shooting prowess. Crew members would throw them as far as they could and challenge me to hit them. I usually could. The Chief Gunners mate couldn't believe how good I was because the ship was never absolutely motionless and did roll a bit even in "calm" seas.

We did have a couple of tragedies on this patrol. The first one involved a dog. One of the ensigns had brought a Scottish Terrier puppy aboard as the ship's mascot. We named it Hooligan, as in (Hooligans Navy—the derogatory term used by the Navy to describe us Coasties). The puppy adapted very easily to shipboard life and was fun to have around. He spent most of his time in "officers country" but was allowed at times to run around the ship.

One day we had a pyrotechnic drill using a dye marker which creates a circle of bright green a few hundred feet wide in the ocean. When the drill was over and we had steamed a few miles away, the P.A. called for any info on the whereabouts of Hooligan. It seemed he had gone AWOL (Absent Without Leave). The crew searched every conceivable nook and cranny on board with no luck. We turned around and steamed back to the dye marker, which took about an hour, with all available hands on lookout for the puppy. I doubt if the poor thing could have swum for that length of time, especially with sharks all about. At chow that night we had hamburgers and some wise guy said maybe they were Hooligan burgers. He got shouted off the mess deck.

The second near tragedy occurred when the Station Easy patrol was over. We had been relieved by another Cutter and were on our way back to Boston. We were to do a sonar anti-sub, search and destroy exercise. First, we launched a large, double-diamond shaped metal sonar target attached with a long steel cable to a tank-like buoy.

Then we steamed off for a few miles and began the sonar search. As an anti-submarine attack ship, we were armed with all kinds of anti-sub warfare equipment. We had a full complement of sonar search gear, hedgehogs, which were contact bombs that were launched high in the air from our bow, and a full complement of K-gun depth charge launchers and stern depth-charge racks. The object of this exercise was to find the target by sonar search, plot a course to intercept, and sink the sub. All course changes were determined by the sonar operator. He was enclosed in the sonar shack and could not see the buoy like the rest of us. All went well and he did a fine job. At the correct moment, we fired the bow mounted hedgehogs and they really fell around the target buoy. Well Done Humboldt!

Then we had to pick up the buoy and the target and that's where everything went terribly wrong. As we approached the target, and slowed to a stop, somehow the cable connecting the sonar target to the buoy got caught in our screws (propellers) and that rendered the ship dead in the water.

The Captain went over the stern in a bo'sun's chair to untangle the mess. Because the screws were under the ship, tucked in under the curve of the stern, it was not easy and the Captain kept getting smashed against the stern by the waves. After what seemed forever he succeeded in freeing the cable and we resumed our trip home.

CHAPTER SIX
New Adventures, New Orders

THERE WAS ANOTHER shooting exercise on the way home. Some of the officers inflated one of our weather balloons, tied it to a long cord flying off the stern rail and were shooting at it with their pistols. We were steaming at about 12 to 14 knots so the balloon was whipping back and forth. They just couldn't hit it. Some of the watching crew shouted: "Smith, show them how to do it!"

I was invited to try, and on my first shot, the balloon collapsed, to the cheers of the enlisted men. I was told that he who shot the balloon had to fill and launch the next one. I did so, and again, none of the officers could hit the damn thing! The officers quickly decided they didn't want to play anymore. They hated to be shown up by a lowly Petty Officer.

By now, after two patrols and four months aboard the Humboldt, I was the envy of much of the crew. They had aptly named me "Rackets" because I had free reign of the ship, no watches, and was able to set my own schedule. I was often asked how my bed sores were coming along. Because I normally went to bed late and slept in, I seldom was in the breakfast chow line. On the rare occasions when I did show up for breakfast, they often let me go to the head of the line in honor of my presence. It was nice to be recognized for my accomplishments! Rank does have its privileges.

The crew knew that the ET's were in charge of the nightly movies that were shown aboard ship. Movie duty was a chore in itself, setting up the projector and the screen, running the movie, rewinding it and then putting all the gear away. The ETs were also in charge of figuring what movies we were willing to trade to the relief ship and making the transfer. We really took a ribbing from the crew from time to time, but it was all part of the game. They knew what we did for them.

Somewhere on the way back to Boston we came upon a drifting life raft. We hauled it aboard and eventually put a wooden scaffold on it, draped it with white cloth so you could see it, sent it adrift, and tried to hit it with our 5-inch deck gun. I wanted to take pictures of my adventures at sea, and I thought this would make a great photo. I went up to the flying bridge, an open space above the main bridge where the Captain is stationed, and just above and to the rear of the 5-inch gun turret.

I got all set with my camera and when that big gun went off, about twenty-five feet away, I felt a huge slap across my face and ended up on my ass. The photo came out fine, albeit a bit blurred. That's how I learned what "muzzle blast" was all about. What an education the Coast Guard provided me! The gun crew never hit the raft target. Although it was a long way away I think I could have hit it with my rifle.

Eventually we arrived back in Boston and returned to the miserable, cold, snowy weather of New England in early February. Again, it was just twenty-four hours from the warmth and sunshine of the Gulf Stream!

Leave was granted to those who were eligible, and it wasn't long before I was on my way to see Fancy in Providence. I got the shock of my life. She kissed me off! I think it was because she wanted to be wooed in a more grandiose manner than this poor sailor could afford. I didn't see her again until thirty years later and boy was I glad she kissed me off! Many things that happen in your life that seem like tragedies are actually the best things that could have happened to you. That kiss off was one of them.

New Adventures, New Orders

Two weeks later, the ship steamed across Boston harbor to an East Boston dry dock for hull repairs. Normally this is a time when the routine is easy and fairly boring. But there were some highlights to being high and dry. One night I strolled up to the bridge and found two or three guys up there and asked, "What the hell are you guys doing here?" They handed me a pair of binoculars and said, "Look over there at that apartment building." After scanning the building I found what had caught their attention ... girls!

The residents of that building apparently thought because their back view looked out over Boston harbor nobody could see in their windows. How wrong they were. After a couple of nights the word spread and you almost needed a ticket to get on the Humboldt's bridge after dark. Every pair of binoculars and ship's telescopes was being used to view these delights. We got to know each resident by their window location. I had never seen a woman douche before, but I had now! The Coast Guard gave this young boy a grand education.

Eventually the repairs were completed and we made the trip back across the harbor to the Coast Guard base. Because my car was still across the harbor in East Boston, I asked for permission to retrieve it. I went across the bay via subway, got in the car and started back to Boston via the Sumner Tunnel. About halfway through the tunnel I saw steam pouring from under the hood. The temperature gauge was at the top. I had no choice but to keep going.

As soon as I exited the tunnel I pulled into a gas station. A quick look under the hood determined that I was low on radiator fluid and that's why it had boiled over. The gas station attendant said he'd add some water. Because it was still winter, I asked if it didn't need some antifreeze as well. He told me that the forecast for the next few days was for above-freezing weather and said I didn't need antifreeze. I'm sure he was just trying to be nice and save a poor sailor a few bucks.

A couple of days later, I cranked up the car and headed out of Boston on my way home for the weekend. I didn't get very far when all of a sudden there was a loud foosh and steam and water began flying everywhere. I pulled into another gas station and after a quick look, I found that my engine block had an eighteen-inch crack with icicles hanging out of it! I was devastated and no idea what to do.

The attendant said I could leave the car there for a day or two and I somehow got home. My Dad took me to our local garage and they offered me a can of DuPont radiator sealer: "absolutely guaranteed to seal any leak or your money back." It cost two dollars. How could I go wrong with a deal like that?

The next day, Dad took me back to Boston. We loaded up the back seat loaded with every kind of water container we could find and the can of super sealer. When we got to the gas station where I had left the car, we started it up and poured the pink gunk into the radiator. Pink juice started pouring out of the long crack in the engine block and I started swearing. A few minutes later my father said, "Kenny, come here!"

When I looked under the hood I was amazed. The long crack was sealed with pink gunk except for a very small place at one end. In another couple of minutes even that, too, stopped leaking. I thanked the gas station operator and we headed for home with Dad and his back seat water supply close behind.

We made the trip without incident and immediately took the car to our local garage. Their advice was to do nothing. If the pink stuff was holding, why mess with a good thing? Just carry some water with you, they said. Any attempt to make a permanent repair was going to be very costly. I opted for the cheap solution and drove the car for many months after that without a problem.

It wasn't long before our in-port time was drawing to an end. It always seemed to go too fast. It was now April and we were next slated to go to Ocean Station "Dog." This station was not quite as far south as Station Easy and a bit closer to the coast of America, but still in the Gulf Stream and warmer than the terrible North Atlantic.

Before we departed the Coast Guard base we headed down the bay to the South Boston Navy base to replenish our munitions. That should have been a nothing event but it wasn't. As we approached the Navy pier, with the Navy sailors waiting to handle

New Adventures, New Orders

our lines, something went wrong or someone on the bridge really screwed up. We rammed the pier, knocking part of it into the water and sending the Navy sailors scrambling for safety! You should have heard what the Navy swabbies had to say and seen the red faces on our bridge. Despite our docking, the Navy loaded up the munitions we needed and we left for Station Dog.

One day in the radar room, while I was chatting with the two radar operators on watch, (air-search and surface-search), the surface-search operator called out: "Radar contact 93 degrees, range twenty miles!" and announced that over the intercom to CIC. It wasn't a big deal because there were other ships sharing the ocean with us and all radar contacts, air or sea, were plotted on our plotting board. However, a few minutes later we had to change course because that other ship was getting too close, and we were required to stay within the boundaries of our Ocean Station assignment.

The "Blip" had been paralleling our course and when we made the required course change, the blip changed course too and maintained it's parallel position. This was not normal! We made a few other course changes, and the blip stayed right with us, just over the horizon. If we zigged, it zigged, when we zagged, it zagged.

Obviously it was shadowing us. Was it a Soviet sub, practicing a torpedo tracking maneuver? Or one of their warships? It could even have been one of ours, also practicing some maneuver. Nobody knew! Everyone from the captain on down was antsy. Remember, there was a Cold War going on, one which could have erupted into a hot shooting war at any moment.

Eventually, after many, many, hours, the ghost ship finally faded away from the radar screen. We never found out whose ship it was. I have always believed it must have been some kind of training exercise for someone. Because who would want to sink a U.S. Coast Guard vessel providing electronic navigational services that all ships in the area were using? The argument sounded logical to me at the time but it didn't make the shivers go away!

One night I was piped to CIC during the middle of the night. There was some concern on the bridge that the bottom of the ocean seemed to be coming up to meet us. We were supposed to be in about 2,000 fathoms (12,000 ft) of water. Someone had turned on the fathometer and it indicated the water was getting shallower.

I checked the instrument out thoroughly and all systems seemed to be working correctly, but the bottom was still coming up. Then suddenly it indicated the depth was getting deeper again and finally we were back in normal water again. I asked the O.D. if we could reverse course and see what happens. He said, "Sure, why not!", so we turned around and sure enough the bottom started to come up again. As we proceeded along, the fathometer traced a perfect mountain shape on the trace paper.

We had found one of the undersea "seamounts" that are now known to be common, forming the Mid Atlantic ridge that runs north to south down the middle of the Atlantic Ocean. Not much was known about that in those early years of the 1950's.

I was determined to increase my Morse code proficiency, so I often spent time in the radio room with the radiomen. These guys were incredible. They listened to one frequency in one earphone, and another frequency in the other earphone, and typed what they heard on both in their log, and carried on a conversation with me at the same time. These radiomen were good, but weird.

To practice my transmission skills, I used to put one of the ships transmitters on the low power "tune" position, ground the antenna to the ships hull, and listen to my dits and dots on one of the receivers. One of the radiomen suggested that I send "BEST BENT WIRE/EE". This sequence is very rhythmic and is a good exercise in cadence for those trying to learn Morse code.

So one night I was practicing my code when the radioman said to me, "What did you just send?" I said, "What you told me to send." And he replied, "Well, you just got an answer because somebody's calling "Best Bent Wire!" I panicked, and said, "What the hell do I do now?" He said to ignore it, which I was glad to do. How the hell could another station hear what I was sending with the transmitter on very low power and the antenna grounded to the ships hull? I guess the Humboldt was a better radio antenna than I thought. I never did that again!

Towards the end of May our time was up on Station Dog and

New Adventures, New Orders

we were relieved and headed back to Boston. We no sooner tied up to the pier when the Captain came into the electronic shop. I was surprised to see him, since he only came down to our shop during rare inspections.

I was even more surprised when the first words out of his mouth were, "Smith, I suppose that you've heard through the grapevine that you are being transferred to the 14th District for Loran duty."

I was floored, devastated, and very unhappy. I said, "But Captain, I've been on the ship for about nine months and now know the ship and my job very well, and I love it here." He replied, "I know, but the orders came from Washington and there's nothing I can do about it."

I was shattered! I had a comfortable position, knew my job, was close to home, and didn't want that to change. I asked if there was anything I could do about it and he suggested I could try a "swap" with another Electronic Technician. But even then, I'd have to leave the Humboldt and take an assignment somewhere else in the District, and I might even get assigned Loran duty in the far north Atlanta. When I heard that, the Pacific sounded a lot better, and I let the transfer go through.

In a few days I received my orders to proceed to Alameda, California, with a ten day leave-in-route. I sold my car to a shipmate for the same price I paid for it (he knew all about the cracked engine block and the pink sealer). I took the train home with my sea bag over my shoulder and I'm not ashamed to report that I had tears in my eyes when I left the Humboldt for the last time.

When I arrived at our summer camp on a lake in Charlton, Mass. I talked to my ex Coast Guard brother-in-law and he said "Be glad you're going to the Pacific rather than one of those freezing northern Loran Stations."

Even as naive as I was, that made sense to me. After all, he had served on a Loran Station in the Pacific called Ulithi Atoll. That didn't mean a damn thing to me but I filed it away, and I'm very glad I did.

That Sunday I went to church with my family. As all young

sailors do, I surveyed the girls in the church and son-of-gun, I spied a girl named Charlotte Ferris I remembered from our Youth Fellowship group at the church. But had she ever grown up! She had been in grammar school when I first knew her but she sure wasn't a grammar school girl now! She had sprouted her "wings" but on her front, not on her back where wings are supposed to be! They maybe weren't big enough to fly, but they were, undeniably, "wings."

After the service was over, I asked her if she'd like to take a ride with me that afternoon. She said she'd ask her mother if she could and would call me. That was the best decision I ever made and I still thank her Mom for allowing her young daughter (15 years old) to go out with this 20 year old sailor.

Our first date consisted of just driving around the local towns looking at the sights. We ended up in a beautiful cemetery that had a large topiary array of bushes that spelled "PRAY FOR US". We didn't know it at the time but apparently somebody did, because it all turned out great for us. I took pictures of Charlotte posing on a tombstone. The next night we went to a movie theater, and did some "necking" in her driveway. The next night we went bowling and did some more necking in her driveway. The next night we went to a drive-in movie and the necking got heavier. And so it went for the rest of my ten days at home. Remember, she was just 15 years old and a junior in high school. It was all very exciting, yet still very innocent. I was still pretty naïve.

My old girl friend Eartha heard what was going on through the grapevine but I never heard from her. I guess I didn't care. When my leave was up my folks took me to the Worcester, Mass. train station for my trip to California and Charlotte came with us. We were waiting in the lower level when we heard a commotion and the Youth Fellowship Group from the church, along with my sister and brother-in-law came barging into the station to see me off. After a few minutes the train was announced.

After the obligatory hugs, kisses, and hand shakes from family and friends, Charlotte and I were locked in an embrace and suddenly the crowd parted and here came Eartha with tears in her eyes. She put her arms around me and kissed me. I really felt like

New Adventures, New Orders

a heel, and if there had been a big enough crack in the platform I would have disappeared through it. I was saved because it was time to board the train. I went straight to the club car and ordered a drink.

Coast Guard Follies

Above: *A sister ship (and identical twin) to the Humboldt on which I served in the North and South Atlantic.* **Below**: *the author as a young ET on his first tour, trying to look like he knew what he was doing.*

Coast Guard Follies

Left: *A typical day on Ulithi Atoll. Sitting in the sun, drinking a beer and thinking about the girls back home.*

Below: *Before heading out to Ulithi, we had a few days R&R in Honolulu. This is the photo from Waikiki Beach I sent home to Charlotte, and I still haven't lived it down!*

Our home away from home: the Loran shack on Ulithi Atoll, surrounded by the antennas. When we decommissioned the station as I left the island, the antennas just crumbled from the rust and humidity.

Coast Guard Follies

Above: *Typhoon, our base pooch, was an excellent hunter of reef sharks, waiting for them to come surfing in over the reef where he'd grab them.*

Left: *our homemade Christmas tree.*

Below: *The local village women getting ready for a dance. After the first week, we got used to their lack of garb!*

CHAPTER SEVEN
Off to the Pacific

AFTER I FOUND my Pullman berth I settled in for the ride to Chicago. This was all a new experience for me and I headed straight for the dining car. The Coast Guard gives you a daily meal allowance while you're traveling. I think it was about $4.00 a day. (Remember, this was 1951)

I perused the lunch menu and the prices blew my mind. I settled for a ham sandwich that cost $.80. That's all I thought I could afford. When it arrived, it was one thin piece of ham between two slices of sandwich bread, cut diagonally across, with a fancy tasseled toothpick stuck in each half. Four bites later it was gone. I saved the fancy tooth picks to send to Charlotte when I got to California.

In Chicago I had to change trains and that meant going to a different railroad station by taxi. The train I rode to the west coast was a local and it seemed to stop at every station, crossroads and shack along the way, just like the train to Cape May. It seemed to take forever to get there but I did get to see the sights in parts of the country that I had never seen before.

When I finally arrived another "Gray Bus" was waiting to take me to the base at Alameda. Seems like you can't go anywhere in the Coast Guard without the obligatory trip in the "Gray Bus".

Off to the Pacific

Like always, I was housed in a "Transient Barracks" along with all the other guys who were awaiting transfer to headquarters in Hawaii. Every morning at muster, they read the list of names of those who were leaving the next day. It was about ten days before my name was called.

While I waited, a friend from boot camp named Ray Alteri and I decided to go to the beach. We took a bus and spent a rather miserable day on a very foggy beach. That night I discovered that, fog or not, I had the worst sunburn of my life. I spent the night wrapped in my blanket, shivering and delirious.

About three days later my name was called to ship out on a troop ship to Hawaii. After the ride in the "Gray Bus" we arrived at the pier and there was the biggest ship I had ever seen close up: the USS General Billy Mitchell. The passengers included enlisted men from all branches of the service and their families. We were herded aboard with our sea bags in tow and assigned a berthing compartment far below decks. The canvas bunks were stacked four high and the guy above me weighed about 250 pounds and his canvas bunk sagged down so far I hardly could fit in mine. As it turned out it didn't matter because I never slept there.

We got under way and passed under the Golden Gate Bridge and headed west towards Hawaii. We had no sooner passed under the bridge before soldiers, sailors, and marines were barfing all over the place. The urinals were filled with vomit to overflowing and the whole below decks part of the ship stunk like you wouldn't believe. I couldn't believe it because the ship hardly rocked or rolled at all. I guess my North Atlantic experience was paying off.

I spent the whole trip out on a weather deck, even to sleep, except to get chow, along with a bunch of other equally disgusted Coasties. It was a four day crossing. On the second day, just before sundown, while they were setting up for the movie on the cargo deck, the ship healed over to port and everyone got excited and wanted to know what was happening. We "Old Salts" told them the ship was stopping at the "Mail Buoy" to pick up and drop off mail. Those dumb land lubbers believed us.

However, that was not the case. We swerved like that because we almost hit a mine! It was a floating mine, sliding within spitting distance by the starboard side of the ship. The word spread like wildfire as we circled around to come abreast of it again. A contingent of Marines was seen double timing towards the bridge, M1's in hand. We pulled alongside the mine and stopped, about 200 yards away.

I had never seen a real mine before and this one was really menacing looking, riding low in the water, barnacles and weeds hanging from it, and those ugly looking detonating spikes sticking up all over. The Marines started shooting at it with no effect. A couple of shots ricocheted off it but nothing happened. It was getting dark and the visibility was getting poorer by the minute.

Then, from up forward, they started to unload on it with a 20 mm. Just about this time, it occurred to me, that if that sucker goes off a lot of people are going to get hurt. The starboard rails were so crowded with people that the ship was actually listing in that direction. I discretely slinked to the rear of the observing crowd. Even from my cowardly vantage point I could occasionally see a 20 mm tracer ricochet towards the sky, but there was no big boom!

By now it was dark and I was spooked because you couldn't see the damn thing. I was hoping that the bridge could see it on radar. A message was sent to COMFLEETPAC about its location and we resumed our course towards Hawaii. Apparently, this W.W. II mine had broken loose from its rusted mooring chain and surfaced, menacing the shipping lanes. Fortunately for us, the ship's lookouts spotted it just in time. My hat's off to that sailor, whoever he was. I've always wondered if the mine was still capable of exploding, and mentally pictured the headlines:

TROOP SHIP HITS WWII MINE, ALL HANDS LOST!

My horrible California sunburn was peeling. I peeled a huge piece from my thigh and put it in a letter to Charlotte and mailed it home when I got to Honolulu. At least she would have a piece of me with her. I thought it was romantic. I'm not sure what she thought!

Off to the Pacific

When we reached Honolulu we debarked and took a "Gray Bus" to another pier and boarded a whale boat to the base at Sand Island. This would be my home for the next ten days. We had liberty every night and it was fun exploring downtown Honolulu. But you had to take that whale boat (the Liberty Boat) to get to the mainland.

One Saturday afternoon I did some shopping for Hawaiian stuff for my girls back home (Mom & Charlotte), and I went to a photo studio to get a formal portrait picture to be mailed home. I paid the guy cash and worried that he might scam a poor sailor, but he didn't, and the pictures arrived at home in good time. When I got back to the Liberty Boat pier, I found I had about an hour wait for the next boat so I went across the street to a nice bar and ordered a beer. I think I had only two, but when the boat arrived and I stood up with my packages, I keeled over and went sprawling on the floor like a regular drunken sailor.

A couple of other Coasties lugged be to the boat, laid me down in the bottom of the boat and then walked me to my bunk when we got back to the base. I awoke in time for evening chow and didn't remember any of this. That Hawaiian beer, combined with the heat, was powerful stuff.

A letter arrived from Charlotte and it was rather bulky. Inside I found a woodchuck tail. Charlotte was an outdoor girl and a good gardener and had a large vegetable garden. Because the woodchucks were eating her vegetables, the elderly man next door had taught her how to shoot the shotgun he loaned her. One day she shot the invading critter and sent me its tail to me to prove her prowess. I believe I am the only sailor who ever received a "Piece of Tail" in the mail.

The best part of this story occurred fifty years later when my neighbor, a former nun, presented me with a birthday present. In the box was a large raccoon tail. Her comment was, "I just couldn't be upstaged by Charlotte and had to give you a "Bigger Piece of Tail!" If there was an ulterior motive on her part, it has yet to be unveiled!!!

Coast Guard Follies

On another day, my buddy Ray Alteri and I took the bus to Kapiolani Park at Waikiki Beach. This was a lovely place and we had a great time and I was careful not to get another sunburn. There was a group of Hawaiian girls sitting on their blanket next to us. At one point, when they came out of the water and were combing their hair, I went over to them and asked if my buddy could take my picture sitting with them. They were very happy to oblige and I snuggled in between them. Ray did the honors with my camera.

I got one of the girls' address (the prettiest one). Her name was Marge Bataoka and we wrote to each other for the whole year I was in the Pacific. When the film was developed, like a damn fool, I sent the pictures home to Charlotte. That was a bad mistake because her letters became few and far between and she was obviously really pissed at me. She said, "You're hardly out of my sight and look what you're doing with those other girls!" Actually I was doing nothing except getting my picture taken at Waikiki Beach but I couldn't convince her of that. I can't imagine why she would have ever thought I was a roving sailor. What could have possibly given her that idea??

Finally the day came when my stay in Hawaii was about to end. I was told to be packed and ready to leave for the airport at a moments notice. The next day I was loaded on the "Gray Bus" again and transported to a military airfield and boarded a MATS (Military Air Transport System) flight.

It was an R4D four engine tricycle gear airplane about the size of a W.W.II B-29. It had canvas, web type bucket seats along the inside of the fuselage and that was the extent of the comforts on board. There was a port-a-potty in the rear. It was not pressurized and we flew at 13,000 feet. To keep a cigarette going was a chore. You had to puff on it continuously or it would go out. We traveled from Hawaii to Johnson Island, a little speck of land in the Pacific to refuel, and then on to Kwajelein Island for another refueling stop, and finally on to Guam in the Mariana Islands. Once there, we were transported to the Guam Coast Guard base, again on the proverbial "Gray Bus".

Off to the Pacific

The base on Guam consisted of a small group of Quonset huts located north of Apra Harbor and the major town of Agana. In 1951 there were many other military installations on the island, but little else. I'm told I wouldn't recognize the place today.

There wasn't much to do. I had arrived with another Coastie who was a Pharmacist Mate and he also was scheduled for Loran duty on a remote station. His name was "Doc" Dilbert and he was from Michigan. We mostly wandered around the small base trying to get used to the hot and humid climate. I found a coconut, complete with it's brown and very dry outer husk, wrote Charl's address on it, added stamps, and put it in the mail. She actually received it. That was not as good as the "piece of tail in the mail," but that was the best I could do. And I'll bet she liked it better than the piece of dead skin!

Now that I was in the 14th Coast Guard District, someone had to decide where I would serve. There was a list of places I had never heard of, and some I was warned against as being no place anyone would want to spend the next year. I remembered my brother-in-law's assignment on Ulithi, so I requested assignment there. I had no idea where Ulithi Atoll was and what that involved, but at least he hadn't told me any horror stories about the place.

On the first Sunday I was in Guam, one of the "permanent party" members of the Coast Guard station took us for a tour of the island in a dump truck. We toured the southern, least militarized part of Guam. It was an education for me to see how the natives lived. They had used excess military building materials to make their homes. Some of them had even enclosed the front part of their "house" to make a bar.

We stopped at one for refreshments and the bartender was a very pretty Guamanian girl about 16 years old. That's when I learned that pretty girls can be found all over the world. My Coast Guard education was filling me with new information no matter where they sent me.

CHAPTER EIGHT
The Ulithi Atoll

MY ASSIGNMENT SOON came through, and I was told I was headed for the Ulithi Atoll Loran Transmitting Station, the assignment I had requested. Even better, "Doc" Dilbert was going with me. We soon boarded a Coast Guard PBY plane for the 340 mile southwest flight to Ulithi, landing on a crushed coral air strip surrounded by thick jungle.

There to greet us was the most rag-tag group of Coasties I had ever seen. They looked like characters out of a Robinson Crusoe movie. They loaded us into an old amphibious "Duck" and we trundled down a path through the jungle to the beach and then into the lagoon. The "Duck" shifted gears to engage the propellers and off we went for the 12 mile, one-hour ride across the lagoon to Potangeras Island, the site of the Loran Station.

Potangeras is a half mile long and about a quarter mile wide. When we ground ashore at the island, the Duck shifting gears to get up onto land and then riding along another jungle path, we eventually arrived at a clearing, dotted with a very neat array of white Quonset huts. This was to be my home for the next year.

LORAN stands for Long Range Aid to Navigation and it was one of the most secret and high-tech developments during WW II.

The Ulithi Atoll

It replaced the old ways, like celestial navigation or radio direction-finding beacons, and was much more precise. Loran stations were constructed all over the Atlantic and Pacific coasts and the South Pacific Islands, operating in pairs with a Master Station and a "Slave Station." The Ulithi station was a Master Station.

It had been constructed in 1945 and consisted of six Quonset huts. One housed four large diesel generators that powered the station, and there was a storage hut, the mess hall and kitchen, enlisted men's barracks, commanding officer's barracks, and the Loran hut & radio room, which was set apart from the other buildings. A towering 110' high Loran antenna and various other radio antennas also stood in our jungle clearing made up of beautiful coconut palm trees and surrounded by the almost impenetrable jungle.

It really was a nice, neat, military "Garden of Eden", but I didn't realize that until years later when I was home and reflected on my military career. Sometimes in life you just don't know how lucky you are!

The manpower on the base consisted of a lieutenant. j.g. who was the commanding officer, Petty Officers, who held the following ranks, engineman, pharmacist mate, boatswain mate, radioman, cook, and seven or eight electronic technicians, who actually ran the station and manned the Loran "scope" watches.

We ET's only stood one four hour watch every twenty four or thirty hours which made for lots of leisure time. The weather was tropical: very hot and very humid. As a result we wore cut-off dungarees with no underwear, no shirts, and Japanese sandals on our feet. All other clothing and everything else you owned and didn't wear was kept in a "Hot Locker," a closet where eight 200-watt light bulbs ran 24 hours a day to keep the humidity down.

Fortunately, the only malady that I brought home with me was a bad case of foot fungus that took twenty years to cure. It rained almost every afternoon in sheets and torrents. If you got caught in one of those showers it felt like you would drown just trying to breathe. These showers usually lasted just five minutes, but they were like a flood from the sky.

Most of the guys stationed at Ulithi were bored stiff, but

not me. I was so interested with the flora and fauna I didn't have enough time in a day for all I wanted to do.

There was the reef and all its fantastically beautiful fish. I went skin diving almost every day, which was like swimming in the most colorful aquarium in the world. The colors of the fish and the other reef creatures were mind blowing. And I got to know the sharks. There were the small tan and black reef sharks (about two feet in length), and the big gray scary ones. Even some of the "clams" that I saw were the most beautiful color of blue I have ever seen.

Topside, I was fascinated with the huge fruit bats. They were the biggest bats I had ever seen. They had a wing span almost three feet across and flew with a slow flapping style, like a crow that wasn't in a hurry. Certainly not like the quickly darting brown bats that we see every evening around our homes. These looked like a small fox with huge wings. They even flew during the daylight hours. They roosted by the thousands on the east end of our island.

And then there were the various lizards that abounded all over the island, and the huge coconut crabs, and the hermit crabs, and the banana trees and other plants that I had never seen before. It was Utopia for me. Unfortunately that wasn't the case for most of the personnel. They seemed to spend most of their time shooting basketball hoops.

Beside skin diving, I also tried to keep myself in shape by working out on a high-speed punching bag almost every day. I really didn't know how to do it but one the other guys showed me how. The punching bag platform was set up on a coconut tree trunk at the edge of the jungle. In that hot and humid climate working out made the sweat come flying off me in sheets that landed in the jungle edge. And that attracted the lizards by the hundreds. They would hear the sweat drops hitting the leaves and thought it was something to eat. Every time I did that, I ended up surrounded with these cute little lizards.

These same lizards hung around the edges of our barracks window screens every night to eat the bugs that were attracted to

The Ulithi Atoll

our lights. They were really fun to watch, especially for an outdoor boy from New England who was interested in all forms of life. These days, every time I see the Geico gecko TV commercials, I'm reminded of those days.

Some military procedures die hard, like 8:00 a.m. morning "Quarters." Our rag-tag group of Coasties, dressed like castaways, had to fall out in our white sailors' hats to salute the flag. The commander then had a chance to say what was on his mind. After I had been there about a month, the Lieutenant announced one morning, "We have a celebrity among us." We all wondered what that meant. Then he started to read a dispatch he had received. It was a commendation for me from Washington for my part in fixing a severe problem with one of the radars on the Humboldt, which had enabled us to stay on station rather than having to have a ship relieve us. Of course I took all kinds of ribbing for that.

That commendation was the only one I received in my military career, but the Humboldt's Captain knew a good deed when he saw one and I was forever grateful for his commendation. But he forgot all about saving the ship from the bilge fire!

The only creatures which detracted from Ulithi's utopian nature were the ants. They were everywhere. We had to set the legs of our bunks in tin cans filled with diesel oil so the ants couldn't climb in bed with us. However, the worst problem was in the head (bathroom). The ants hung around the toilet and if you've never been bitten on the anus by a hungry red ant then you don't know what a "pain in the ass" really is!

Poor dear Eartha was still writing to me every week and in every letter she asked me "How's the weather in Hawaii?" I kept telling her I wasn't in Hawaii but thousands of miles south of there in a place called Ulithi and included a map with my letters. It didn't matter. The next letter from her still started, "Dear Ken, How's the weather in Hawaii". I finally gave up. All the other girls that wrote to me knew where I was, but Eartha just didn't get it, even though she had the right address. I doubt if she knew where Kansas was.

We were not totally isolated on our base. Indeed, walk out of any of our buildings and you'd be in the native village that bordered our station. There were about two dozen natives living on Potangerus Island with us. Most of the natives lived on the larger islands. I was fascinated with the native culture and language. All of the natives on our island were very friendly and I quickly became fast friends with many of them and they helped me with my quest to learn about them.

It took me a long time to learn their language, but fortunately many of them spoke pidgin English so we could communicate. This was all fascinating to me and I spent a lot of time with my friends, sampling their food and absorbing their way of life. They were some of the finest people I have ever known. They were calm without a hostile bone in their bodies. I can't imagine what they thought about us. But they often came to watch our movies in the mess hall, so I imagine they often compared the Hollywood American with the real thing.

The native women dressed from the waist down in a skirt that they called a Hoopla and the men wore a "G-String" that looked like a modern-day thong. All those naked breasts were quite a cultural adjustment for a 20 year old American boy. Boobs were everywhere and in the first few weeks my eyes got sunburned. After that, the excitement wore off, and one paid no attention. And breasts were not sexual objects to the natives. They were only used for feeding babies. What a waste! I can still remember Josephine, however. She was only about twelve years old, but she had a pair that were incredible. They absolutely defied the laws of gravity and stuck straight out! I knew of no law of physics that could account for this engineering marvel.

Aside from my duties as an Electronics Technician, I was very interested in medicine, so I often helped our Pharmacist Mate with his chores, which included providing medical care for the natives. I gave shots and even sutured cuts. But my biggest medical memory was the day I painted those fantastic tits.

There is a disease in that part of the world called Yaws. It looks like poison ivy, but is far more serious. And as my good luck would have it, Josephine one day came down with Yaws on her

The Ulithi Atoll

boobs and reported to sick bay. "Doc, "our Pharmacist Mate, didn't have any treatment for Yaws except to put Calamine lotion on the affected parts to stop the itching. Now Doc was a very happily married man, so in the true spirit of "Semper Paratus" I came to his rescue and offered to treat this poor young lady.

With the utmost of care and tenderness, I carefully and slowly administered the pink Calamine lotion to the affected mammary glands, trying not to get my drool mixed with the lotion. When the medical procedure was finally concluded, I stepped back to admire my handiwork (and God's). My paint job was so beautiful I felt like Picasso. It was probably the most "Tit"-a-Lating experience of my military career.

I just had to photograph this incredible sight for future reference. The now painted boobs looked like the business end of a pair of ballistic missiles. As I write this, more than fifty years later, I'm sure those fantastic boobs have reached the ground by now, because gravity will have its way. But it doesn't matter because I was there to see this ninth wonder of the world. The color pictures I took are still in my possession. Copies are $19.95 plus $5.95 shipping and handling (plus a 10% surcharge for dirty old Radiomen).

About every three months we would throw a party for the natives. How they knew about it I don't really know, but apparently the Ulithi community grapevine worked very well. Natives from all the other islands around the lagoon would sail over in their canoes. The lagoon-side beach looked like a Wal-Mart parking lot with the canoes pulled up on the beach.

We made our own liquor, which we and the natives called "Screech". We made it by dumping large cans of fruit that we had on hand—cherries, peaches, whatever—into a large wash tub in our storage hut. This brew would ferment, foam up, overflow to the floor and finally end up covered with a tan crust. When the crust formed, we knew it was done.

We scraped the foam off, strained out the solid stuff, and what was left was a slightly milky liquid. It was quite tasty and had the normal alcoholic effect. The natives loved it, but only the men drank it, never the women. (That was a shame!) Once, we found a dead rat in the brew. We just threw him out and never mentioned that poor critter. He either drowned or died of alcohol poisoning, but he did have a smile on his face. I'm sure the alcohol content killed any bacteria the rat may have harbored.

We strung lights around the base so the festivities could go on into the night. The natives donned their "formal" dress, which consisted of fancy headdresses made of bird feathers, flowers, and palm fronds, and skirts for both the men and women. They all wore fancy and complicated ornaments and anklets of many designs, made from coconut palm fronds. Both the men and women performed their native dances, but separately, never together. They used no music, but chanted in cadence with the dance routine. My Ulithi language expertise wasn't good enough to tell whether they were actually singing a song or just chanting. Maybe it was just as well that I didn't know what they were saying!

The children were always put at the end of the dance lines, where they could participate and learn without messing up the rest of the line. The women did a fantastic dance which I called the "Stick Dance". It would have made a military drill team look shabby, and the clicking-sticks rhythm would have made a great song.

Watching the women dance with their jiggling boobs, of every shape, size, and "dangle angle", was something to behold. They would have put Hooters out of business! These parties went on until the wee hours, and everybody had a good time. Most importantly, it was a break from the usual routine, both for us Coasties and for the natives as well. We all looked forward to these galas.

As usual, our regular chow was generally great. Our cook (Cookie) was a southern black man. One day he decided to make chili. We all sat down at the mess table with these large bowls of chili in the middle. After a short while, Cookie, standing behind the kitchen counter asked, "So how's the chili?" Some of the guys replied, "You call this stuff chili! Where the hell did you learn to make chili? Where we come from we make four-alarm chili with plenty of red pepper in it. This stuff is like baby food!" I didn't know what

The Ulithi Atoll

they were talking about. For my New England taste buds, it was already too hot. But I ate it anyway and washed it down with a cold drink to put the fire out.

Time passed and a few weeks later Cookie decided to try his chili again. Except this time he tried to please the dissenters and give them what they wanted. Or maybe it was his way of retribution. In any event, the chili was put on the mess table as before. This time, after a few minutes had passed, Cookie asked the troops how they liked the chili. The wise guys could only mumble it was fine, as the sweat rolled down their faces. After one mouthful my mouth was on fire! You needed an asbestos mouth to eat that stuff! But the complainers would never have admitted that. Cookie stood in the kitchen with the biggest toothy ear-to-ear grin I've ever seen. Payback can be very pleasing! That night I went into the native village and dined on fish and coconuts! Moral of this story: If you're in the military, don't bitch about the food, unless you're the cook.

There was the day an officer from the fuel supply ship came up to our mess hall for a bite of noon chow. Seeing Cookie behind the mess counter, and assuming he was one of the Ulithi natives, the officer said: "You makie me san-wich?" in his best pidgin English, while he gestured with his hands about how to make a sandwich. Cookie just gave the officer his famous wide, golden toothed grin.

So the officer did his whole act again. Finally, Cookie responded, in perfect English, "And what would you like on it, Sir?" The officer was so embarrassed, and the fact that we were laughing our heads off didn't help him one bit.

CHAPTER NINE
Ulithi Follies

AFTER I WAS at Ulithi Atoll for three months, we had a change of command. The young Lieutenant j.g. we started out with was replaced with another, except this new guy was an old fart. He was what is known as a "Mustang," which in military parlance means an old officer who didn't graduate from the Coast Guard Academy and probably would never advance in his rating. He was from Falmouth, Mass., out on Cape Cod.

He was a big fat thing so we called him "Lard Ass". This man was bad with a capital B. I recall many horror stories about this guy, but will only relate two of them. He was the type of man who gives all officers a bad name, and he's lucky he wasn't found washed up on the beach. He was the worst thing that happened to us on Ulithi.

The Beer Caper

Shortly after I arrived at Ulithi, we received a bad lot of flat beer from the San Miguel brewery in the Philippines. The fresh water on the island was brackish and not fit to drink, so we used either coconut juice or beer for our daily liquid intake. We sent a letter to the brewery explaining the problem and heard nothing for about three months. One day, when we made the twelve mile trip across the lagoon to meet the supply plane at the landing strip, we found an extra ten cases of beer that we hadn't ordered. "Lard-Ass" informed us that the extra beer was his, he had ordered it "special." Not knowing any better, we accepted this.

About three months later, one of our ET crew got sick, and an emergency flight was dispatched to Ulithi to transport him to a hospital in Guam. When he had recovered, and was sent back to the base on Guam, one of the Coasties there asked our man how we liked the "free" beer we had received from San Miguel as a replacement for the flat stuff we had complained about. The truth was now out. That lousy Lard-Ass had stolen our beer.

We didn't dare confront him for fear of retaliation. When you're stuck on a remote island with no other recourse, you keep your mouth shut and just survive!

The Chess Match

I had always wanted to learn how to play chess. Shortly after I arrived at Ulithi, I found one of the other ET's played the game and he agreed to teach me. We played while we stood our scope watches. It wasn't long before my chess teacher's time was up and he rotated back to the States, leaving me without a chess partner.

One night at chow, while I was on watch in the Loran shack, Lard-Ass announced from his private table in our mess hall (he wouldn't sit with the rest of us) that he was looking for a game of chess, and did anyone play? In unison the group chorused, "Smith does!"

The next night at chow, Lard-Ass spoke. "Smith, come to my quarters after you eat and I'll whip your ass at chess." Believe me, it wasn't a request, it was an order! So I went, and got my ass whipped. He roared with laughter and wanted to know what ever made me think I could play chess. Of course, he told everyone else about his victory, along with his degrading laughter.

We played twice more with similar results, but in the fourth game the tables were turned. As the game progressed I looked at the board and noted, in stunned disbelief, that if I simply moved my queen it would be check mate. I studied that move for a long time, because if I was wrong, I knew the bastard would forever humiliate me. All the while he's saying, "For Christ's sake, will you move?"

Finally, with heart racing, I moved my queen and meekly said, "check mate." He was stunned. "What? What?" he cried, peering at the game board. After a series of "harrumps," he acknowledged my victory. And decided he didn't want to play anymore.

I probably set some kind of speed record getting back to the mess hall to tell the guys, but they didn't believe me. I was never "invited" to play chess with him again. In fact, Lard-Ass never mentioned chess again. It was only then that the guys believed that I had really beat the old bastard!

The Sinking Ship

The next thing this dumb "Commander" did was sink the LCM. In the summer of 1951, our station received a used World War II LCM landing craft. This replaced the old, worn out "Duck" we had been using to make our weekly crossing of the lagoon to the air strip for our rendezvous with the supply plane. I have no idea how Lard-Ass wangled such a deal. He was only a Lieutenant. jg and the only weight I could see that he pulled was his own fat ass. In any event, we got it and it was the pride of our commanding officer. It may have been the only thing he ever commanded that floated.

The water over the lagoon reef was far too shallow to bring the LCM ashore, so it sat at anchor, off the reef, on the lagoon side of our island. It really did make the 12 mile trip across the lagoon a pleasure, compared to the wallowing old duck.

One evening a few weeks later, after chow, I walked down to the beach to contemplate my navel. It wasn't the beautiful type of evening you normally associate with the tropics, as there was a storm brewing. The lagoon wasn't peaceful looking, but badly riled up by the impending storm.

Suddenly I noticed that the LCM seemed to be riding very low in the stern. Lard-Ass had ordered it anchored stern to the wind and waves because that was where the mooring bollards were. As I watched for a few minutes I could see that the waves were washing over her stern. There was little doubt: she was sinking, by God!

I ran up through the village and into the mess, shouting to our boatswain, "The M-boat is sinking, The M-boat is sinking!" He didn't believe me and made remarks about stupid ET's being too late for April Fools. I finally said "O.K., if she goes down, remember, it's your ass because I told you." He said, "Oh for Christ sakes, I'll go look!"

So we walked back down through the village and when we got to the beach, he took one look, and started screaming "the M-boat is sinking! The M-boat is sinking!," and ran like hell back to the mess hut. Everyone not on watch ran down to the beach, including the Lieutenant.

It was getting dark, so someone was dispatched to bring our weapons carrier down to the beach, so its headlights would provide some light. Lard-Ass asked for volunteers to row our 18-foot skiff out over the reef to the LCM. Four of the best oarsmen among us, which included me, plus one of the young native boys, manned the oars and the rest pushed the boat down to the water. Our engine-man manned the "sweep" oar, and was the coxswain who steered the boat.

All went well until we reached the edge of the reef. The surf was really crashing over the reef edge and we had to get through this without broaching. We bided our time until we studied the wave sequence, picked the right time, and gave it all we had. We made it, but it was a hell of a ride!

When we reached the side of the LCM, we all scrambled aboard and had the native boy hold the skiff's bow painter. We didn't want the skiff tied to the LCM for fear of them both going down. The engineman pulled the rear engine compartment hatches and it was instantly apparent that she was a goner. The water was about even with the tops of the two engines. We all started grabbing what ever we could salvage, fire extinguishers, tools, lines, etc., throwing them into the skiff.

Coast Guard Follies

Suddenly, someone shouted, "she's going down!" And damned if she didn't, right from under us, in a hundred feet of water. We all dove for the skiff and scrambled aboard.

Now we had to get back to shore in one piece. Now that we were facing the beach, the weapons carrier headlights were blinding us. We yelled and hollered to turn them off, but of course, they couldn't hear us due to the roar of the surf. It was one wild, surfboard ride back to the beach, but we didn't broach, and all hands were accounted for, very wet, tired, but otherwise O.K.

I never saw the official report of this incident. I'm sure it would make interesting reading, and I'm also sure it didn't jibe with my telling! None of us who risked our lives to try and save the M-boat got a thank you, let alone a letter of commendation! And poor Lard-Ass... his one and only floating command...and it sunk! How would you like that on your record? Serves him right!

A few weeks later Lard Ass had another one of his "brilliant" ideas. We were going to raise the sunken LCM from 100' of water! We were instructed to build wooden frames that would each hold six empty 55-gallon oil drums. Each of these rafts would have a scaffold and a hole over the middle where we could run a stout line down through the center of the raft to the LCM. The theory was that when the lines were tightened and the tide rose, the buoyancy of the drums working together would lift the LCM a bit, and it would drift towards shore. This would be repeated on each tide, and the LCM would slowly work its way to shore. I never figured out how the hell he planned to get it up over the 90-foot reef edge with only a three foot tide. Either he had never heard about advance planning or he had a secret plan that he kept from us. I was smart enough to keep my mouth shut about this.

After all our hard work, and after the natives made 100-foot free dives without busting their eardrums to the LCM to attach the lines, the whole plan stalled because it didn't work. Gee, what a surprise.

Ulithi Follies

Service Interruption

There was another major screw-up while I was stationed at Ulithi that really affected our operation. When you are stationed on a remote Loran Station in the middle of the Pacific Ocean, you learn that most things are done in a routine manner. Part of the reason why is the "military way," but the truth is that conditions are such that rarely are there any occurrences that would inspire anything to change the routine. And so it was at the Pacific Loran Transmitting Station, Ulithi Atoll.

Our laundry was done on a certain day by one of the native boys, the supply plane came on Thursday (if we were lucky), the two Loran transmitters were switched on Saturday and the off-line transmitter was serviced, and the station was "fueled" on Friday. That routine was always the same, except once.

In the wee hours of a Saturday morning, I was on scope watch in the Loran shack, half asleep, dreaming about things back home. Suddenly the Loran timers went bananas, the transmitter went off the air, and the lights faded out. This wasn't totally unusual. Because the equipment was old and tired, it occasionally went on the fritz. We had been trained by the engineman on how to start up a new diesel generator and put it on line to minimize the "off air" time. It was much more efficient than running to the barracks and waking the engineman and having him do it.

So when things went haywire, I ran to the generator hut, where the four diesel generators were housed. By the light of my battle lantern, I looked at the control panels to determine which one had been on-line and switched it to off-line. I went to the next generator and started the gasoline fueled "pony" motor, and then put it in gear to roll the big generator over. It caught right away, with a clatter and roar. I increased the throttle and brought its speed up to produce a nice 60 cycle output voltage and then shut the pony motor off. Just as I switched the generator on-line, the damn thing wound down and died. There I was in the dark again, now with two dead generators.

Coast Guard Follies

I went to the next generator line and repeated the procedure, and just as I cut that one on-line the same thing happened. By now, I was frustrated and couldn't figure out what the hell was wrong. I repeated the start up procedure on the last generator and, you guessed it, that one went bye-bye too.

We had now been off the air for about fifteen minutes and I was panicked. I ran to the barracks to wake up the engineman. His name was Stan. As soon as I told him that the station was without power, he started ranting and raving about the "damn ET's" and the fact that he had taught us how to start generators and what the hell had I screwed up now, and on, and on. I kept trying to tell him that I had started a new generator, in fact all of them, and they just kept quitting, but he wouldn't listen to a "stupid ET."

We both went back to the generator hut, and while I held the light, he attempted to start a generator. It wouldn't start. So he tried another, and another, and another, with the same results. About this time, his seaman/engineman/striker showed up and stood there looking sleepy and stupid. This guy was a goof-off if there ever was one. Stan turned to him and said, "You did fuel the station today...didn't you?" With a look exactly like that of a kid whose hand is caught in the cookie jar, the striker said, "I forgot."

Chief Engineer Stan went nuts! Barking orders to the goof-off, they jumped in the truck and headed for the fuel dump at the far end of the island, where our fuel was stored in 55 gallon drums.

They came back with a drum of diesel fuel and started putting the fuel in the tank. Stan went inside and began cranking up a generator. It wasn't easy because the fuel lines were dry, but eventually it started. I ran back to the Loran shack and began the transmitter restart procedure. This takes about four minutes. By now we had been off the air for more than 30 minutes. Unheard of!! That was a new record, and not a good thing. Finally, the electronics settled down, the transmitter was back on the air, and our slave station was able to get back in sync.

I have no idea how this fiasco was handled officially, as I never saw the documentation, but it seemed as though some heads should have rolled. Mine didn't, so I didn't care much. I guess the

Ulithi Follies

lesson is "Semper Paratus" (Always Ready) unless you have a goof-off in your crew!

A Shocking Experience

I suppose the closest I came to death, other than the LCM sinking incident, was getting electrocuted. One night I was fast asleep in my rack dreaming of girls back home, with a fan at the head of the bunk blowing down the length of my body to keep the mosquitoes off. Suddenly someone was shaking me and saying , "Come on Smitty, time to go on watch." (Oh how I hated those words.) The midnight-to-four watch, having done his duty, was now about to hit the sack, leaving me to get to the Loran hut before something went wrong. He wasn't supposed to leave his watch until his relief got there, but that wasn't the way we did it at Ulithi.

I pulled on my cut-off dungarees and sandals and headed out into the dark for the 100-yard walk to the hut. The Loran hut was a rusty seven-year-old Quonset hut (nothing lasts long in that humidity). Housed inside were two 100,000 watt transmitters, one in operation, and the other in standby mode. Inside a double copper-wire screened room stood the two Loran timers.

These were six feet high by four feet wide, with a metal edged desk across the front. There was a wicker chair and a 12-inch fan on the floor. And a goose neck desk lamp sat on the desk. Now this was no ordinary lamp. Somewhere in its past, the reflective metal globe had become loose and some enterprising ET had soldered the globe to the lamp socket, which meant that to change the position of the reflector, you had to twist the goose-neck itself to get the light to shine where you wanted it, and herein lies the tale.

As I entered the Loran timer screen room, I was blinded by the desk lamp on the table. The reflecting globe was turned out to face the room instead of down to face the table. The bright light was more than I could handle at that hour of the night having just been roused from a deep sleep.. So I grabbed the goose neck with my sweaty hands and started to twist it to the desired position. My bare, sweaty legs were pressing against the metal edge of the timer desk.

Coast Guard Follies

    I felt a tremendous electrical shock and was propelled backwards, ripping the lamp's electrical cord from the socket, falling backwards over the wicker chair, and landing on the floor. My dog tags were on a metal bead chain and they flew out and were grabbed by the fan on the floor. The fan wound itself up to my face and twisted my head to one side and stopped turning. Fortunately, there was a metal guard around the blades, so it didn't mess up my pretty face. It sat there humming and the dog-tag chain was choking the life out of me. I was really stunned and didn't know which end was up. My immediate concern was to begin breathing again.

    Somehow I got one arm to move and I felt around for the fan's power cord and gave it the biggest yank I could muster. It was enough to pull the plug out of the wall. The fan stopped humming and backed up a bit, enough so I could breathe.

    There I lay, mostly paralyzed and afraid I was going to die. There was a signal button that sounded a klaxon horn for help, but it was far out of reach. As my senses and my mobility slowly returned I was able to unwind my dog tag chain from the fan. I gradually got myself into a sitting position and just sat there, while I surveyed my situation. I decided I wasn't dead and wasn't about to be, so I got up on shaky legs, turned the chair upright and sat down. I tried to decide if I should blow the klaxon and summon help. If I did, the rest of the crew would either be pissed that I got them up, or laugh at me, so I decided that discretion was the better part of valor and just sat there feeling sorry for my self.

    I finished my watch and suffered no ill effects, other than a nice welt on my neck from the chain. The next day I took that damn lamp apart and fixed the shorted wire. If we had had a spare, I would have gladly deep-sixed that thing off the reef. Occasionally, I see one of those lamps and a chill runs through me, even 50 years later.

CHAPTER TEN
Island Life

EVERY WEEK, THE supply plane would arrive at the air strip across the lagoon. It was twelve miles across the lagoon to Falalop Island, where the landing strip was, and usually our boatswain, engineer and any off-duty ET would make the trip.

Because Ulithi lies only 9° above the equator, we had two different seasons: hot and humid and sort-of hot and humid, with clouds and rain. The cloudy, rainy season often caused a problem for the supply plane. If the cloud ceiling was below a certain level, they would not descend to find our island, let alone the air strip. And this weather pattern often was the spawning ground for a typhoon. When the wind was up, we couldn't get our boat off the island because of high surf breaking over the reef. During one stormy spell, we went six weeks without any supplies or mail. No cigarettes, toothpaste, toilet paper, or food. These are the essentials of life! So I went native.

The native diet consisted of fish, coconut meat, papaya, breadfruit, and taro root. As a native New Englander I loved fish, and the natives had more ways to cook fish than you can imagine. The simplest way was to just toss it in the fire. They didn't gut their fish; you just ate the meat from around the body cavity. Sometimes they rolled the fish in large "elephant ears" leaves and buried them under the coals of the fire and steamed them. Either way, it was delicious! But they couldn't get over the fact that I wouldn't eat the fish eyes. They'd say, "Smitty, you no eat eyes? May I have?" They'd pop them out with a finger, slurp them down and say, "Moo Mi", (very good). I ate in the village a lot, but I never could do fish eyes, even though I was brought up eating raw clams.

The natives' cigarettes were something to behold, and even more of an adventure to smoke. Each man and woman carried, in their purse, a pouch of "tobacco" and torn strips of newspaper about nine-inches square. The tobacco was little kernels of something that looked like what we kids in New England used to call "Indian tobacco." The paper was creased along one side and the tobacco dispensed from the pouch into that creased groove, one kernel next to another kernel, for the whole length of the paper. Then the paper was rolled up, western style. Lighting one of these "cigarettes" was something to see. They flared up like a torch and you had to quickly blow out the flames. I never realized just how bad my tobacco addiction was until I smoked one of those and found myself enjoying it! I guess desperate men do ridiculous things.

When things got really critical with our supply situation, it was decided the PBY would do an air drop. This was one of the days the plane could land but we couldn't get off the island. They flew over Ulithi at about 500 feet and dumped out five packages with parachutes. Naturally, they all landed in the ocean. Bomber pilots they weren't! So it was back to the fish and the "Roman Candles" cigarettes for another week. Somehow, we all survived.

About the Ladies

I quickly learned that on Ulithi, there are all kinds of different customs dealing with male-female relationships. For instance, Ulithi women don't kiss like we do—lip to lip, except young girls who were taught by the Coasties. A kiss to most women was really a big sniff. You put your arms around the person, went cheek to cheek and took a big sniff, sort of like one dog checking out another.

Island Life

Even when the Catholic Padre came to the island, the natives would drop to one knee and sniff his ring.

Another custom involved menstruation. When the women had their period, they would be banished to the Blood Hut for the duration. This is not uncommon in other cultures around the world. The Blood Hut was set off to the side of the village at the edge of the jungle. Usually there were a few women in there at the same time but young twelve-year-old Josephine seemed to be out of sync with the other women and she was afraid stay there alone. So she would ask me to stay with her at night, often with a few other young kids as well. Being a good guy (like all Coasties!), I kept her company, sleeping on a hard coconut mat with rats crawling around.

A somewhat strange sexual custom was a prohibition on touching a women's genitals with one's hands. I imagine this was because contracting any kind of vaginal infection out in the tropics, far from medical help, might mean death. So what at first seemed strange really makes sense.

And then there were the "Push-Push" ladies, Yagamar and Harriet. The Ulithi natives were dark skinned and hard to see in the dark. Often, during the evening, I would be sitting on the beach with some of our guys and the native boys, telling sea stories, when all of a sudden in my ear, I would hear a whisper: "Smitty, Go push-push?" It didn't take a rocket scientist to figure out what that meant. Naturally, being a good ambassador of the U.S. Armed Forces, I would slink off into the boonies to oblige the lady with a little "Push-Push". The things that we military men had to do for our country! And my wife Charlotte has always wondered how I became such a good lover. In reading this account, she learned that the "Push-Push" training was just part of my Coast Guard education, under the heading "Semper Paratus" or "Always Ready!" Which I suppose is another definition of "serviceman!"

Radioman

Our Radioman "Sparks" held skeds, or radio schedules, with Guam (NRV) three times a day, so he was never off duty for more than four hours at a time during daylight and thus he was always moaning about his terrible lot in life.

Back then, a Coast Guard ET was expected to be able to copy Morse Code at 10 words per minute in order to earn promotion to Second Class Petty Officer. I wanted to raise my classification from ET3 to ET2, so I would spend some of my off hours in the radio shack practicing my code, with help from Sparks. Of course, I never realized that Sparks had a devious plan in mind for all his help.

When I got my skill level up to 10 w.p.m., Sparks suggested I sit in with him and try to copy along on his next sked. Gee, I thought, that would be fun. (I can't believe I was that dumb and couldn't see what was coming!) After a few more of these "lessons," he asked me one Sunday if I would take over his noon sked so he could make a trip to one of the neighboring islands. I didn't think I was ready, but he assured me that it would be a piece of cake. There's little traffic on Sundays, he said, my skills had improved and besides, the radioman on Guam would slow down for me. It was, of course, all b.s.—he just wanted some time off.

By the time the fateful Sunday arrived, I was a wreck and scared to death. I reported to the radio shack (a screened room that was part of the Loran Hut) about an hour before sked time and started practicing what I would send and watched the clock count down to the witching hour, as the sweat flowed off my body. Finally, at precisely 1200 hrs, with a trembling hand I tapped out the message: " NRV NRV de NRV3 NRV3 ZBO P QRS 10 ET." (QRS 10 ET means "please slow down to 10 words per minute because an electronic technician is at the key.")

The operator at the other end immediately acknowledged and instructed me to send my traffic. So I sent my "P" traffic (weather report) and he rogered it and then said he had two for me. I almost died! One of them turned out to be some kind of commissary inventory shipment order, full of lists and numbers. I was trying to copy all this down in longhand because I couldn't type. I'd get behind and break in on his sending and ask him for "AA" (all after). He'd start again. I could almost hear the disgust in his sending fist. He'd start out at 10 wpm and gradually speed up to his normal cadence.

Island Life

By the end, I'm sure he was as frustrated as I was. I had my scribbled long hand copy, covered with sweat drops, and he probably was anxious to get on with his other chores. But we finally managed to reach the end. I still had to type this all up on a message form by the hunt and peck method. That was a chore in itself. It was a traumatic experience to say the least. However, after a few weeks cooling off period, I was conned into doing it again and I seem to remember it went a little better.

Several weeks later, the radioman's tour was over and he rotated back to the States. Lard-Ass informed the district HQ that they needn't send a new radioman right away because he had an ET who could handle the duty. So there I was, screwed again! Eventually a new radioman showed up and that was a big load of my shoulders. Again, no thanks, no commendation, no nothing.

In hind sight, I guess my baptism by fire wasn't all bad. Six years later (1958) when I was a civilian, I decided to become a ham radio operator, the CW (code) part of the exam was a piece of cake. No FCC code test could be worse than that first day on a live key at Ulithi. I'd still like to kill that "Dit Jockey" at Guam for not being nicer to a struggling ET who was way out of his element.

Holidays

In December of 1951, the weekly PBY supply plane from Guam delivered a Christmas tree. This was the sorriest tree we had ever seen. It was completely brown and the needles were falling off. We appreciated the gesture but there was no way we were going to put that in our mess hut. So, like a lot of things you have to do in a far away place, we improvised. We took a wooden broom handle, drilled holes in it, attached coat-hanger wires cut to the right lengths, and draped those wires with the green crepe paper and the ornaments that had arrived with the tree. The picture of that tree is priceless!

Decommissioning

In the early months of 1952, the Coast Guard decided that the Loran Station on Potangeras Island had run its course and was about to fall apart. They got no arguments from me! Headquarters decided to build a new station on Falalop Island, where the airstrip was, and a civilian construction crew flew in and began work.

The new station had nice concrete, air-conditioned buildings instead of our rusty old Quonset huts. To us, it seemed like they were building a luxury resort! There would be no more trips across the lagoon for the new Coasties. It all was so nice, one could almost be tempted to stay for another year (no way!).

Eventually the new station was ready to go. We conducted Loran tests with them and finally the day came in the month of May 1952 when we shut down and they took over our Loran duties. At that point we were to "decommission" the Potangeras facility and prepare to leave. The only thing we did was to take down the 110 foot antenna for fear that it could hurt the natives. That wasn't too hard. The antenna was so old and rusty, it just about crumbled. We left the buildings and equipment for some other crew to recycle.

Finally the day came for us to leave. Our ragtag group crossed the lagoon by boat for the last time. Some of us, including Doc Dilbert and I, were headed for home. The other guys were going to be reassigned to new stations.

Homeward Bound

The supply plane took us back to Guam and the Gray Bus was waiting to take us back to base. Doc and I were only there for a few days under orders to be ready to leave on two hours notice to Hawaii. Even though you were assigned for a specific flight, any higher ranking officer could bump you off the flight. Enlisted men were low on the totem pole.

Doc and I went to the local commercial airport on Guam and bought our tickets to get home once we arrived in California, whenever that might be. After hanging around a couple of days, we finally arrived at a military airfield in Hawaii.

Now that we were back in civilization we had to wear our uniforms for the first time in a year. Boy, did that ever feel weird. A day or two later, the Gray Bus took us to the airfield and we were on our way to California. We landed at a military airfield and took

Island Life

a cab to the Coast Guard base. We got our orders signed and were out of there in two hours flat. We went to a railroad station to ship our sea bags home, and then to the commercial airport for our flights home. When we said goodbye at that airport, Doc and I thought we'd never see each other again. But that turned out not to be true.

When I finally arrived at Worcester Airport my folks were waiting for me and took me to our summer camp out on the lake in Charlton, Mass. where I was going to enjoy thirty days leave. However, it wasn't a summer camp any more. During my year away, they had converted it into a year-round home. It was beautiful, but it was also miles away from "where the girls were!"

My Dad had just purchased a new 1952 Chevy that very day and he wouldn't let me drive it. So there I was stuck in the wilds with no transportation. The very next day he took me to a car dealership and I bought the 1950 Chevy that he had traded in for the new one. It took a day or two to get it registered and insured and finally I was ready to go back to my old stomping grounds where the girls were.

To tell the truth, I had no real idea which girl's house I was going to stop at first. I made the fateful decision to stop at Charlotte's house. She had just graduated from high school and was now free to date. She and I began spending more and more time together.

CHAPTER ELEVEN
Endings and Beginnings

AFTER MY THIRTY days were up, I drove to the Boston Coast Guard base and checked in. I was interviewed by two officers for assignment. While looking over my service record, one of them said, "Smith, how come you're still a 3rd class ET? Your service record doesn't show that you screwed up."

I told them that I had served at Ulithi under Lieutenant Lard-Ass (of course, I used his real name!) and that he had never advanced anyone in rating while I was there. The officer got a big smile on his face and said, "Smith, you are now a Petty Officer 2nd class." I guess "Lard Ass" was well known all over the world. I suspect my not being advanced in class was due in large part to my having beaten him at the chess board.

Because I only had a few months service time left on my enlistment, I was assigned to the electronic repair shop at the Boston base. This was nifty duty because we had liberty every day and almost every weekend. This shop serviced all the electronics in the entire district. That encompassed all of New England from Maine to southern Connecticut, and the shop was mostly staffed by civilian

Endings and Beginnings

technicians. I had other duties, some on weekends, like the holiday parades, shore patrol, and guard for the local brig. In that job, I would take four or five inmates out on work details and if any of them got away, I would have to serve their time. That was not going to happen on my watch!

We always brought the inmates back from their work detail for chow just before the chow line was open for the rest of the base. I had to guard them while they ate and then return them to the brig for lockup before their afternoon detail began. When they were locked away in their cells I could go to get my chow, and by then the mess hall was nearly empty.

One day, I grabbed a tray and hustled down the chow line where I found a large vat of what looked like clam chowder. I took a big bowl and sat down to eat. It was delicious but I did notice some very small red crabs floating in the chowder. I had never seen little red crabs in clam chowder before. But it was so good I went back for more. I told the cook I'd like another bowl of that wonderful clam chowder and he said, "That ain't clam chowder, it's oyster stew!" I almost choked. For all of my 22 years I had hated oyster stew because when I was about five years old my mother had made some for lunch and I didn't like it and she made me sit there for hours and eat it all. So I spent 17 years hating something that was really delicious. Mom's rules aren't always right and can sometimes end up giving her kids some funny food hangups.

After a few weeks back at the base in Boston I was walking up the stairs with a couple of buddies after chow, and this officer came up and greeted me like a long-lost brother. It was Lard Ass! I totally ignored him and kept walking.

My buddies said, "You just blew off that officer!" I replied, "Yes I did and you don't want to know why." Fortunately, I never saw Lard Ass again, except to read about him in the local newspaper about some cockamamie scheme he had to acquire an island off the coast of Cape Cod. I don't know if he ever succeeded in buying that island, but I'll bet if he did, it probably sank!

Coast Guard Follies

A California Adventure

One day in October, while working in the electronic shop, I heard the PA system summon me to the office. I was told that I was being sent to a Navy Sonar School in San Diego, Calif. "Are you nuts?" I said. "I only have a few weeks left on my enlistment. What would they do that for?"

Of course, the answer was that Washington had requested two ET2s to the school, and there were only two of us available. The military works in strange and stupid ways sometimes. I pissed and moaned so much that they said they'd send us on the TWA Ambassador flight. I didn't know what that meant, but it did make the long trip easier. Beginning at the airport in Boston, when the other ET and I were ushered into the VIP lounge and treated like royalty!

When we boarded the plane we walked down a real plush red carpet, with red velvet ropes on brass stanchions along the sides (This was in the days before enclosed jetways, and all passengers had to walk outside onto the tarmac to board a plane). It was a TWA Constellation, one of the fanciest planes of its day, equivalent to the Concorde SST. The other passengers were obviously either rich or government officials and I'm sure they wondered how a couple of "swabbies" rated a trip on that flight.

Shortly after reaching altitude, the stewardess came by and asked if we'd like a bottle of Champagne. Did she really have to ask?? A while later she came by again and saw that the bottles were empty and asked if we'd like another. But of course! I next remember waking up as we were descending into Los Angeles for our connecting flight to San Diego.

When we arrived in Los Angeles we had a couple of hours layover for our flight to San Diego, so we strolled around the terminal. We were approached by two guys in Zoot suits, very Hollywood, wanting to know if we would be interested in being on television. My buddy said "No way," but I waded right in and asked what I would have to do. It turned out that they produced a show for travelers from the open-air airport lounge, and I could call anyone I wished on the phone. In those days, TV was live with no taping or delays. The show started and I was introduced by a stunning girl in

Endings and Beginnings

a flight attendant's uniform.

The emcee asked me what the insignia on my sleeve was for. I saw the camera dolly in for a close-up and could see in the monitor that my "crow," with the double circle helium atom, filled the screen (see insignia on inside title page).

"Well, we're not supposed to tell this," I said seriously, "But I'm a flying saucer pilot!" There was an audible gasp from the audience. UFO's were a hot topic in the early fifties.

Then it was time for the phone call. He asked who I wanted to call. "My mother," I said. "Not your girl friend?" he asked. I replied, "No, I'd be embarrassed if she wasn't home." That got another giggle from the audience.

When my Mom answered, I immediately told her to watch her language because we were on TV. I finished the conversation with Mom, off camera, and when I returned, they were shooting a live coffee commercial. The camera again dollied in for a close up of the coffee can sitting on a lace doily on a little table.

Being the curious type I am, I always wondered if they used real products in those commercials, so I reached over with one hand and turned the bottom of the can up towards the camera. Sure enough, the bottom of the can had been cut out, and it was empty. The crowd roared with laughter and the emcee went spastic. They quickly got me out of there. That was the end of my television career.

During the show, a fellow came to me with a note, saying this man had called the TV station and wanted to speak to me. The address meant nothing to me but I thought it may have been a friend of my sister's from when she was in California. After the show was over I called the number and found out it was a very rich gay guy offering to have his chauffeur pick me up and return me to the airport. I begged off, saying my flight was leaving soon and I didn't have time. If it had been a gorgeous female movie star that called, I might have accepted!

Eventually we got to San Diego, took a cab to the Navy base and checked in. And we were again assigned to the transient barracks. Some things never change. This place was the pits, compared to the Coast Guard barracks I had seen. By morning, we were both fed-up with this place.

They did weird things there. I kept hearing the PA system talking about "Mustard on the Grinder". To me, a grinder was an Italian sandwich, and why would the PA be telling people to put mustard on one? I soon learned that they were saying "Muster on the Grinder." In the Navy, a Grinder is a parade ground.

At 0800 hrs sharp, we presented ourselves at the base office. We gave the Yeoman our orders with a twenty dollar bill tucked inside, and asked him if he could get us out of there. I told him that I only had three weeks left until my scheduled discharge. He consulted a book and found a regulation stating that one must have at least three months obligatory time left on your enlistment to go to a Navy school. That sounded good to us, as my traveling buddy only had six weeks.

The Yeoman went over to a Lieutenant at another desk and after a minute, the Lieutenant hollered over to us, "Do either of you want to ship over?" (That meant re-enlist for another hitch.) We just laughed. We were told to come back at noon and they'd have new orders for us.

When we returned, we were ordered to proceed to the nearest Coast Guard unit, which was the Air Rescue Station, just down the street from the Navy base, for further assignment. We were glad to get off that lousy Navy base.

The next few days were spent digging dandelions from the base lawn while the messages flew back and forth from Boston to San Diego, as the brass tried to decide what to do with us. We did get liberty at night and I met one of the fellows that I knew from electronic school and he took us out on the town. That's when I first saw pizza being made by twirling the dough in the air until it was the right size. That was amazing to this rural New England boy. Wow--the stuff you learn in the military!

We finally got orders to return to Boston. We had our return tickets on that wonderful TWA Constellation, so off we went to make our reservation. We arrived at Logan airport in Boston in the early afternoon, but timed our arrival at the base until after liberty time. It was a Friday, so they gave us weekend liberty passes and we went home.

The following Monday morning was the day of reckoning. But nothing happened, except there were a lot of red faces around the base office and the rank and file thought it was the greatest caper they ever heard of. It was pretty much a total waste of a week, but the fancy plane ride was nice.

Ending and Beginnings

Finally, on December 12, 1952 my active military career came to an end as I received my discharge from the active Coast Guard, and was relegated to the inactive reserves for three more years. All in all, my three years in the Coast Guard has always been one of the greatest adventures in my life and I don't regret any part of it. The education I received was priceless. And I don't mean just the formal electronic education, but rather the things I learned about myself and the people from all walks of life that I came in contact with. I'm sure my mind aged and matured more than just those three years.

On January 2nd, 1953 I applied for a job at the Harvey-Wells Electronics plant in Southbridge, Mass., the next town over from my hometown. I was hired as a Research & Development technician. About six months later, I got Charlotte a job there as the Engineering department secretary. The following February 19, 1954, on a Friday, we were married. I used my mustering out pay, and what little savings I had acquired, to buy a house in Charlton. This was our love nest and that's where we spent our honeymoon because we were too poor to do anything else.

A year or so later, to our great surprise, we received a phone call from Doc Dilbert, the pharmacist mate from Ulithi, and found he had been transferred to Boston. He and his family began to visit us on weekends and we did a lot of reminiscing about the good old days in the South Pacific. This poor guy was still in the Coast Guard, being transferred around the world doing his duty, with his family in tow. That was exactly why I didn't want to be married and still in the military.

Coast Guard Follies

The years flew by. We spent our leisure time hunting, fishing, boating, camping, and we raised beagles. In 1958, the horrors of the Morse code episodes at Ulithi finally paid off. I passed my Amateur Radio license test with no problem and received the call sign K1ICM. A year later Charlotte also passed the exams, and her call sign is K1JEA.

It was such a wonderful life that after fifteen years we split our assets down the middle and got divorced. A bit more than a year later, we realized we had made a mistake and started dating again. Looking at the calendar, I noticed that our wedding anniversary, Feb. 19th, would also occur on a Friday. So we retraced our steps and got married again on the same date, at the same time. That sure made it easier than trying to remember two separate anniversaries.

I retired from active industry at the tender age of forty three, as production manager of one of the major integrated circuit manufacturing companies. As I noted earlier in this story, little did I know back in 1951 that the announcement about that transistor discovery would have such a huge impact on my life. The integrated circuit became the great grandson of the transistor and is now used in just about every electronic device we own, and has just about replaced the vacuum tube, which I was brought up on.

Charlotte got in on the very ground floor of the computer industry when they were still using "punch cards" and she built her career in that field.

I'm now in my mid-70s and we've been married more than 50 years. And our story hasn't ended yet. We both look forward to the next chapter, and trust it will be as happy, interesting and entertaining as the ones that came before.

CHAPTER TWELVE
Postscripts

Just because the funny stuff in the Coast Guard ended doesn't mean that all funny stuff in my life went away after I was discharged. Humor—and humorous adventures—continued to be part of my life and career. Here are some examples.

My first civilian job was at Harvey Wells Electronics. Young R&D engineers don't seem to get enough enjoyment from their profession, so they often resort to some sort of merriment to liven up the often dull atmosphere in the laboratory. Naturally, I was often a ringleader!

Our chief engineer Louie was deep in a development project that wasn't working properly. He had the malfunctioning pieces of equipment upended on his lab bench, with cables and wires of every sort running this way and that to a multitude of test and measuring equipment stacked on and around the bench. Our lab benches were placed back to back in long rows and each had a shelf attached to the rear where one could stack test equipment, power supplies and other stuff. We usually thumb-tacked the schematic drawings to the top edge of the shelf to keep it handy for quick reference. This is the set-up Louie had.

Coast Guard Follies

Now as any experienced electronic engineer knows—and most everyone else can imagine—any piece of electronic equipment that begins emitting smoke is extremely bad news. Having experienced this myself in previous disasters, I thought I had a great idea for a practical joke of Louie.

At lunch time, when Louie was out of the lab, I found a piece of clear plastic tubing and snaked it from the opposite bench, through Louie's maze of wires and inserted one end into an inconspicuous corner of Louie's project. Everyone in the lab, of course, was in on the gag.

After lunch, we all went back to work and Lou continued to delve deep into his problem. After a while, I wandered over to the bench behind his and tried to look like I was doing something constructive. He couldn't see me anyway because of the big schematic he had hung up. He was busy anyway, shutting off the power, replacing a component with some other piece, turning the power back on, observing the results, making notes and doing the whole thing over again. You know...he was working!

I lit a cigarette and when Louie turned the power back on the next time I blew a large puff of smoke through the tube. The results were spectacular! The smoke came curling up through his components in a most realistic fashion. When he saw the smoke begin to curl over his bench, he reacted like any normal, well-educated engineer would—TOTAL PANIC accompanied by an unprintable oath! He jumped for the power switch, somehow got tangled up in the maze of wires and cables, and accidently pulled some of the equipment on his bench shelf off onto the project and onto the floor.

All of the other engineers came running to see what had happened and if Louie was OK. We helped him pick up the pieces and assess the damage. When all was restored, Louie began checking out his project carefully, trying to find the burned component. But of course he found nothing. He spent the next hour rechecking his notes and calculations. When he was satisfied that all was well, he turned the power back on and kept close watch on the meters and dials looking for any sign of smoke.

Satisfied that all was normal, he busied himself on the calculations for the next component change. While he was distracted, I blew another puff of smoke through the tube, and got another panicked dive for the off switch from Lou.

This went on for another two or three cycles until someone at the other end of the lab couldn't contain himself and began to snicker. Louie, who luckily had a great sense of humor, finally realized he had been "had" and wanted to know who the &%$#$ was who set him up. Of course, I was long gone, having taken myself off to the machine shop for something important. If Louie had caught me, I believe I would have been fired. But he eventually saw the humor in it and I was able to continue my career without loss of life or limb.

I think the moral of this story is the world needs more people like Louie and fewer idiots like me. And, unfortunately, I still smoke. You'd think I would have learned my lesson.

Playing God

MY AMATEUR RADIO hobby also provided an outlet for my humor and other funny stuff over the years.

One day, I was tuning around the six-meter amateur band looking for foreign stations (DX). Finding nothing of interest, I aimlessly tuned down below the band edge of the ham band and, to my surprise, heard a conversation taking place. After listening briefly, I determined this conversation was between a young, newly married girl and her mother, both talking on their cordless phones.

The girl was speculating on what her new husband would get her for Christmas. I just couldn't resist. In my deepest, most ethereal voice, I said 'HAVE YOU BEEN GOOOOOOD?" There was a long silence and then the girl finally said "Who is this?" I replied "THIS IS GOD!" To which she replied, naturally I guess, "Oh, my God!" and hung up.

I sat there chuckling and I remained tuned to the frequency. Sure enough, five minutes later, they were back and the mother said "Who was that?" The girl replied "He said he was God." With that, I jumped in again and said "IT IS GOD AND I'M LISTENING ALL

THE TIME." They both exclaimed in unison "Oh, my God!" and hung up again.

I'm sure that if these two ladies told their friends and families about their miraculous encounter that the local churches were overflowing the next Sunday. Just call me Ken the evangelist! (And to the FCC: this is purely a fictional account and any resemblance to any persons living or dead is purely coincidental!).

Paprika Balls

MY WIFE CHARLOTTE and I have always enjoyed the outdoors: hunting, fishing and camping. During the 1960s, it was an opening day ritual to fish a lake in East Brookfield, Mass., with my buddy Harold in my boat. This type of fishing didn't come anywhere near to satisfying the purist in my, but in view of the usually high stream conditions at that time of year and Harold's lack of prowess with the bamboo wand, it seemed like the right thing to do. We usually trolled a variety of streamers or spinning lures and usually caught about 30 or 40 trout between us, keeping the twelve largest.

One cold April opening day, about ten in the morning, we pulled the boat onto the beach to stretch our legs and have a cup of coffee. The beach had the usually complement of shore-bound anglers with their spinning rods and forked sticks. When they saw our stringer of 14- to 15-inch trout, they all crowded around and complimented us on our expertise. One fellow said to us "Every time I looked at you guys it seemed you had one or two fish on. What were you using?"

That's a common question from one fisherman to another, of course, but for some reason I decided to get a little weird. To this day, I have no idea why I said what I said, or where the thought came from, but I replied "paprika balls." Two or three of the shore fishermen immediately exclaimed "PAPRIKA BALLS? What the hell is that??"

Well, every good fisherman knows the hard part is to get the quarry to take your offering. Then, all you have to do is give him a little line and play him a bit. So, being the expert that I am, I did just

Postscripts

that. Wearing my best disgusted look, I said "Don't you guys keep up with the news? You must have read in the paper that the state hatcheries have been adding paprika to the food pellets they feed the fish to enhance their color and make it hard to tell a native from a stocked trout?"

The eyes of one of the fellows brightened, and I knew I had him. I kept playing the line. "Stop and think," I said. "These fish have been eating pellets flavored with paprika all their lives, so that's all they know. What better bait could you use?"

I got a chorus of "Yah, right" and "Of course!" I noticed my buddy Harold had walked away. Some guys just don't have any guts!

The next question from "Bright Eyes" was obvious. "Where the hell do you get paprika balls?": he asked.

"You don't get them, you make them," I said. I paused for a moment, then continued. "I promised the fish biologist I wouldn't tell anybody about this, but you guys seem really interested, so I guess it's OK."

By now, the crowd was pressing in close and a couple of other guys from down the beach came running up. By now, I had no idea what words were going to come out of my mouth next. But sometimes you just have to throw your brain in neutral and wing it. So I did,

"First of all," I said, "You need paprika. Not a little, but a lot. Like about a case of the stuff. Take a large bowl and mix all the paprika with enough white vinegar, some corn meal and a dash of Worcestershire sauce to make a thick soup. Take some cotton batting and pull it apart into very small tufts and put the tufts into a shallow baking pan. Pour the paprika mixture over the cotton and bake it in a 200 degree oven until it gets to the consistency of soft rubber. Then, when the pan cools, cut the stuff into small squares and mold it around a number 8 or 10 hook with your fingers. Put the balls on a cookie sheet and bake at 275 degrees until they are hard. Store in the refrigerator. That's all there is to it," I concluded, "It's a bit messy, but you've seen how well it works, so it's worth it.

During my lecture, you've never seen eight grown men in more rapt attention. It was as if I was revealing the secret of eternal life to them, I suppose when you think about it, a secret lure is close to that for a fisherman.

Can you imagine the mess and smell in all of those kitchens? I wouldn't dare guess how many divorces my recipe caper might have caused. But I accepted all their thanks and smiles, wished them good luck and went off to find Harold.

When we were back in our boat and away from shore, Harold asked "How the hell could you keep a straight face while you were telling them all that crap?"

"I guess I'm just a natural born liar," I answered.

You might think the story ends there, with the smug feeling one gets after pulling a fast one. And so did I. But two weeks later, we were at a different lake not far away for another try at the trout. Again, we came ashore in mid-morning and again, there was a group of fisherman on the beach.

I asked one of them how he was doing. "I haven't had any hits," he said. "You gotta have paprika balls."

That just goes to show you can't keep a secret lure secret for very long! I wish I could tell you that paprika balls really do work and the joke was on me, but I moved away shortly thereafter to Rhode Island.

Number, Please

I suppose there's a fine line between humorous and nutty, and after a lifetime of skirting along the edge, I got so silly in my old age that my wife Charlotte couldn't stand me anymore and had me put away in the Veteran's Home in Bristol, RI.

On my first day in the "home," I felt really lost and alone. I was in a ward with about 25 other unbalanced former servicemen and I spent the day wandering around with nothing to do. Later that evening, shortly before lights out, things really got confusing. Someone at the other end of the ward shouted "427" and everybody laughed. Somebody else hollered "319" and they all laughed again.

Postscripts

I didn't know what was going on, so I turned to the fellow in the next bunk and asked "What's with the numbers? Is this some kind of game you fellows play?"

My neighbor answered "Hell no, it's not a game. They're telling jokes."

This made no sense to me, so I said "I don't get it. What's so funny about those numbers?"

"Look, fella," my neighbor said, "Most of us have been in here a long time and we never get any new jokes, and we get sick of hearing the old ones over and over. So we've typed up all the jokes and put them in a book. Each joke has a number, so if you want to tell a joke you just call out the number and if they like it they laugh. It sure saves a lot of time."

"You've got to be kidding me!" I said, amazed.

"I'm not kidding," he said. "Tomorrow, go out to the nurses' station and see the book for yourself."

The next morning after breakfast, I went to the nurses' station. And sure enough, there was the joke book. I spent the rest of the day reading and chuckling over some of the stories. I found a couple jokes that really tickled me, and committed the numbers to memory. I figured I'd use them that evening to help break the ice with the other guys.

That night, just before lights out, I figured this was the time. I sat up in bed and hollered "97!" Nobody laughed. I was humiliated and slunk down under the covers. I turned to my neighbor again and asked "What went wrong? I remembered the number, and it was a good joke. Why didn't they laugh?"

My neighbor replied, "Well, you know how it is...some people can tell a joke, and some people can't!"

At this writing, I'm happy to report that I have returned home, almost fully recovered, except now I go around telling old jokes by the numbers and people like you are the ones to suffer for it!

EPILOGUE

IN RETROSPECT, I think the education I received in the Coast Guard went far beyond mere electronics. I learned so much about people from all walks of life and that understanding has helped me throughout my life. I hold my Coast Guard experiences as one of my greatest assets, even fifty-six years later.

I'm sure that my Coast Guard adventures and Charlotte coming into my life are the greatest things that ever happened to shape who I am today. And I owe a special thanks to all those people mentioned in this story, from the Coast Guard officers, my fellow crewmen, the wonderful native people, my various girlfriends, and my parents. Without their influence I would not be the person I am today.

Glossary

GLOSSARY

Word	Description
Bowswain Mate	In charge of rigging, lines, anchors, small boats, etc.
CIC	Combat Information Center (ships brain center)
Cookie	Military cook
Coxswain	Small boat man in charge.
Duck	Amphibious military truck (DUKW)
Ensign	Lowest ranked commissioned officer
ET	Electronic Technician

Coast Guard Follies

LCM	Landing Craft....Mechanized
Lt. j.g.	Lieutenant junior grade. One rank higher than Ensign
LORAN	Long Range Aid to Navigation
M-1	Military Rifle of the 1940's & 50's.
O.D.	Officer of the Day
O.O.D.	Officer of the Deck
O.S.V.	Ocean Station Vessel. Also known as a "Weather Ship"
PBY	Two engine amphibious airplane
Petty Officer	NCO....non-commissioned officer
Pharmacist Mate	Nautical medic
Powder Magazine	Ammunition & high explosive storage
Quarters	Same as Roll Call or Muster
Quarter Deck	Rear quarter of a ship
Radar	Radio Direction and Ranging
Sonar	Sound Navigation and Ranging

Glossary

Shore Patrol   Navy or Coast Guard military police

Sparks   Radioman

Stern Racks   Depth Charge launcher....stern mounted

Surf Boat   A large row boat used along the coast

Surfman   Those who manned the old Life Boat stations

Swabbie   Sailor

Weapons Carrier   Larger "Jeep" type of vehicle

Weather Deck   Open air exposed deck

Yeoman   Clerk or secretary

www.ingramcontent.com/pod-product-compliance
Lightning Source LLC
Chambersburg PA
CBHW071833290426
44109CB00017B/1817